(Continued from from. , ,.)

about it; we make the acquaintance of Mrs. Aino Sibelius; and we are told about the friends and visitors, and even about the attentions of a burglar. During long years Mr. Levas has seen what the life of a world-famous composer is like, and he gives a marvelously graphic account of it.

Music-lovers will be especially drawn to the chapter "The Creative Artist," in which Sibelius speaks of his vocation as divinely inspired. For him, composition was "brought to life by means of the *Logos,* the divine in art." Sibelius always, says the author, particularly wished to emphasize that all his seven symphonies were pure, absolute music, and exclusively fashioned from within, from his own musical ideas. They had no programme element at all—although many people believe that they have—and all the thematic material was his own. Another fascinating chapter tells of Sibelius's favorable attitude toward modern music, especially that of Bartok. He knew Schoenberg's dodecaphonic system well, though he never made use of it.

Santeri Levas has here presented a warm and rounded work on Sibelius as man and artist.

SIBELIUS

a personal portrait

SIBELIUS

>>>>>>>>>>>>>>>>>> > >>>>>>>>>>>>>>>>>>>>>>>>>>>>>>>>>>>>

a personal portrait

SANTERI LEVAS
translated by Percy M Young

Lewisburg
BUCKNELL UNIVERSITY PRESS

Library of Congress Catalogue Card Number: 73–11556

ISBN: 8387 1411 0

PRINTED IN UNITED STATES

PREFACE

❯❯❯

This book about Jean Sibelius is a shortened version of a comprehensive biography in my own language, which I published soon after the death of the great Finnish composer. The biographical material has here been concentrated into a brief *curriculum vitae,* while the individual and the composer—as I had come to know him as his secretary over two decades—has been placed in the foreground. While engaged on this work I have all the time kept before me the fact that I am here writing particularly for foreigners.

There is no detailed examination of the master's music in this book, but only a brief discussion of the principal works in a simple and comprehensible manner without recourse to theoretical terminology. On the other hand I have considered everything important that the composer himself had to say to me about music and artistic creativity—especially his own.

It has, however, been of the greatest concern to me that I should always give prominence to the purely personal aspect. I hope therefore that my readers will have at least a more or less accurate image of the Finnish composer. It is widely recognized that Jean Sibelius is reckoned among the great creative spirits of our time. But as a man he was also of a wholly rare kind; brilliant, original and charming, and at all times full of concern and affection for his fellow-men. To write about him was for me a real joy.

S.L.

Helsinki.

CONTENTS

⊳⊳ ⊳ ⊳⊳⊳⊳⊳

PLATES

All the photographs, with the exception of that by Yousuf
Karsh, were taken by the author.

The publishers wish to express their gratitude to Mr Douglas Pudney, Classical Promotion and Repertoire Manager, E.M.I. Records, for his contribution *Sibelius and the Gramophone* and for the Select Discography.

INTRODUCTION

⇒⇒⇒

A brief biography

Jean Sibelius was born on 8th December 1865, in Hämeenlinna, a small provincial city in the south of Finland. At his christening he received the names Johan Julius Christian, but all his life his relations and friends called him Janne. As an artist he used Jean as his Christian name—never Jan as is sometimes stated.

When he was two years old his father—Christian Sibelius, the city and regimental doctor—died of typhus, a victim of his calling. His mother, Maria Charlotta (*née* Borg), was the daughter of a parson, and very religious. She devoted herself to her three children, Linda, Janne and Christian, with true love and self-sacrifice. Soon after the death of the father the family moved into the home of the maternal grandmother, Katarina Borg, where the composer to be was to spend his childhood and his school-years.

He went to the first Finnish grammar school [1] in Hämeenlinna, which counted among its pupils a number of important men, among whom was President J. K. Paasikivi. Janne was in no way a model of industry or propriety. His whole nature was much too restless, and his imagination too lively, for him to be able, day by day, obediently to finish his school exercises and to submit to the rigorous discipline. Sometimes during his lessons he was so deeply immersed in his own thoughts that he hardly knew where he was. He liked mathematics and nature study, but everything else at school was a nuisance to him. When he was an old man he said: 'I look back for the bright spots in vain.'

[1] Until 1809 Finland was under Swedish rule, and for many decades afterwards Swedish was almost exclusively the language used in all institutions of higher education.

Although his school did not provide much pleasure for him his childhood cannot be described as joyless. He took a lively part in the games and escapades of his companions, and there was much that made for fun in the pleasant little town. Everyone knew everyone else; there was never any lack of sociability in the evenings; and in the better-class homes chamber music flourished. Then there were the beautiful surroundings of the town, which provided an inexhaustible source of pleasure for the boy. He went into the woods a great deal, with a gun on his shoulder; not only on account of the game, but much more because he always felt in such good form among the silent trees and mountains. The love of nature awoke in him early and was to stay with him all his life.

The children were fortunate in the family circle. The grandmother was strong-willed, but at the same time she always appreciated a word in jest. So far as the unmarried aunt—Julia Borg—was concerned, the children represented a substitute for all that had been denied to her. In the summer months the family stayed in Loviisa on the Gulf of Finland with their other grandmother, Katarina Sibelius (also a widow), who was unable to say no to any of the children's requests. Their aunt Evelina Sibelius, who liked good music more than anything, was even less disposed to deny them what they wanted. Their only uncle, Pehr Sibelius, for his part used to take the two boys with him to Turku (about 150 kilometres west of Helsinki) during the Christmas and Easter holidays. He was a well-to-do and highly esteemed—if somewhat eccentric—bachelor, who occupied himself a great deal in his free time with music and astronomy.

Early on Janne's character showed qualities inherited from his parents. Dr Christian Sibelius had been a kind-hearted man—taking life as it came—who had a large number of friends and would never willingly miss any gregarious evening party. His son had the same engaging character. Even when he was a schoolboy he stole all hearts, for like his father he was gay and amusing. But an emotional sensibility, inherited from his mother, made him variable in disposition. It took very little suddenly to change his cheerfulness into moroseness, which, in turn, was as quickly dispelled by a friendly word. The boy also inherited his keen sense of imagination from his mother. In hours of solitude he used to like to linger in an inner world, far removed from everyday reality. Even when he was a boy he perceived in nature and in humanity much that was hidden from others.

To his mother therefore he owed the emotional impressionability and fertile imagination that were necessary qualities for a great composer. But he also in the main derived his musical talent from her. It is true that a good deal of music was played and sung in the father's family, but the Borgs should be regarded as the principal source of musical interest. This was the view of the composer himself. His relationship with his mother was always very close. Long after her death, even in old age, he sometimes had the impression that he was under her unseen protection.

Sibelius was no child prodigy like Mozart and Mendelssohn, and at first no particular attention was paid to his musical gifts. The whole family was musical, and in those days it was a matter of good form to cultivate music in the home. Nobody took any more notice because the ten-year-old boy was beginning to compose little pieces.

But at the beginning of 1880, when he was fourteen, music took hold of him with unusual power. He had been given a violin as a present and after he had begun his lessons he was so much affected that everything else lost its attraction. He was a quick learner and was soon in request for playing at school functions and private soirées. In the woods, however, it was a large stone that sufficed for a concert platform, and at Loviisa he used to like to stand up in the sailing-boat and to play to the murmurous waves. He dreamed that one day he would be a great violinist.

Chamber music had a quite exceptional fascination for him. It was practised in almost all the best families to a greater or lesser extent, and at home he had a trio of his own—his brother Christian playing the cello and his sister the piano. At first these young musicians were satisfied with the classical composers, but soon they turned to the Romantics—Schubert, Schumann, Mendelssohn and Brahms. The musical utterances of the great masters, which he was now zealously getting to know, provided a course of study of which the value for the budding composer can hardly be over-estimated.

The boy's love of music inevitably resulted in school lessons becoming more of a tribulation than ever. He remained in the fifth class, but in spite of this he completed his course and passed his final examinations in 1885. For the sake of his family he matriculated in the Faculty of Law of the University of Helsinki. But that was about all he did towards an academic career. At the same time he began to attend the Conservatory of Music (now known as the Sibelius Academy), and after two terms he gladly dropped Law so that he could at last devote himself to music. The family had given consent with heavy hearts.

He studied with Martin Wegelius (1846–1906), founder and director of the Conservatory, who was not only a good teacher but also a good friend to him. Wegelius had immediately recognized the rare gifts of his pupil. Under his capable direction the young Sibelius learned musical form, harmony and counterpoint. He also had a violin instructor at the Conservatory, but very soon it became apparent to him that he was not a born virtuoso. He had an altogether too unruly temperament for that, and in any case he was already too old. In 1889 he brought his studies to an end with a string quartet in A minor and a Suite for String Trio. Both works gave so much convincing proof of originality and of rare musical talent that as a result it was easy to obtain a grant for the young composer to go abroad.

In the winter of 1889–90 he studied in Berlin, under Albert Becker (1834–99), a somewhat dry theoretician who was then one of the top people in music in the city. Next winter he went to Vienna, where he was taught by Robert Fuchs (1847–1927)—the so-called 'Serenade Fuchs' [1]—and Karl Goldmark (1830–1915). He felt himself very much at home in the Imperial City, where, indeed, he even used to frequent Pauline Lucca's [2] salon, and he heard a lot of good music.

In the meantime, in the summer of 1890, Sibelius had become acquainted with his future wife, the nineteen-year-old Aino Järnefelt, and in June 1892 the young pair were married. At that

[1] His best-known works are five serenades for strings.
[2] A famous Austrian opera singer.

time Sibelius was already teaching theory at the Conservatory in Helsinki.

By now his name was known to well-informed people in Finland, for at the end of April 1892 he had had his first large-scale work—the symphonic poem *Kullervo* (for soloists, male voice choir and orchestra) performed in Helsinki. This event was not only a milestone in the life of the young composer but also in the musical history of Finland. For the first time a composer had appeared, with a strong personal style and, at the same time, Finnish characteristics. He was clearly influenced by the Romantics, but the individuality of his music was unmistakable.

Kullervo is a wide-ranging programmatic work with strong dramatic implications. It tells of the fate of a tragic hero in the *Kalevala*—the national epic—from which Sibelius was later to draw inspiration for further important works. *Kullervo* was enthusiastically received, but before long it ceased to satisfy its creator. After four performances Sibelius withdrew the work, considering—not without some reason—that it needed a complete revision. That, however, never came to pass. *Kullervo* was played for the first time since its original performances in the summer of 1958—against the expressed wish of the recently deceased master.

The young composer, however, had now made his breakthrough and he devoted himself to fresh undertakings. In the autumn of 1892 the first of his important orchestral works, the tone-poem *En Saga*, had appeared. Cecil Gray, the well-known English musical writer, said of this that it represented the entry of Finland into musical history.[1] *En Saga* is not, as is sometimes said, based on any national epic material. Sibelius himself suggested that its atmosphere recollected rather the Icelandic *Edda*. But otherwise he said that *En Saga* was no programme work, but should be understood as an expression of a spiritual condition that embraced almost his whole youth.

En Saga, which Sibelius revised in 1901, showed him already to be a master. In its original form it was romantic, richly scored and opulent, whereas the second version is significantly shorter and more severe; but both bore witness to a rare originality and

[1] Cecil Gray, *Sibelius*, 1931, 2nd edition, 3rd impression, 1943. p. 71.

creative power. The poet Elmer Diktonius beautifully characterized *En Saga* as 'simple as a folk-song, wild as the wilderness, and splendid as the princess and the half of the kingdom'.

In the following ten years, as well as a large number of smaller pieces, the principal works of Sibelius's romantic period were published: the suite *Karelia*, the four *Lemminkäinen* legends, the tone-poem *Finlandia* and the first two symphonies. The much-loved incidental music to Adolf Paul's tragedy *King Christian II* in suite form also belonged to this period and—its culminating work so to speak—Sibelius's only concerto. This was the violin concerto in D minor, which was slow in finding a place among the most frequently performed concertos, but which now belongs to the repertoire of every virtuoso. From 1905, the year of the Violin Concerto, we also have the little *Valse triste*. Released from its first function as incidental music this is played all over the world, and next to *Finlandia* is doubtless Sibelius's best-known work.

While the *Karelia* suite and *Finlandia* were composed for national occasions [1] and the *Lemminkäinen* legends were based on material from the *Kalevala*, the two symphonies were in no way conceived with programmes in mind—although it is often stated that they were. They belonged to a period in which Finland was defending herself against oppression on the part of the Russian giant. For this reason it has frequently been taken for granted that the composer has given expression to his country's fight for freedom in his symphonies. This is valid insofar as Sibelius—like every other Finn—was deeply conscious of the anguish of his people, and this could not have been without influence on his frame of mind and his music.

In the First Symphony Sibelius confronts us as a full-blooded Romantic, but this does not prevent the work—like every other work written by him—from having an unmistakable Sibelius imprint. It is melodic, richly orchestrated, strongly emotional, and dramatic; from time to time—as critics have often observed—it is reminiscent of Tchaikovsky. Sibelius himself would also not deny

---

[1] *Karelia* was composed for a pageant that took place during 1893 to illustrate folk-art and -history. *Finlandia* was composed with similar intention in 1899, and the present work belonged to a suite.

a certain influence from the Russian composer—'... if I am quite honest', he used to say. With the First Symphony Sibelius finally crossed over to the province of absolute music, in which he was to accomplish his real life's work.

The first performance of the First Symphony took place in Helsinki early in 1899 and was a tremendous success. No longer was there any doubt: Finland had a composer of international stature. His standing in his own land was firmly secured. He received a life pension from the State and was able to live independently as a composer. At the turn of the century his name also came to be known abroad.

In the summer of 1900 Sibelius was lucky enough within a short space of time to have his works played in a number of European countries. For this he had to thank his best friend Robert Kajanus (1856–1933), founder and conductor of the Helsinki Philharmonic Orchestra, who was one of Sibelius's most important champions. On the occasion of the Paris Exhibition in 1889 Kajanus undertook a long tour with his orchestra, which took in the three Scandinavian countries, and Lübeck, Hamburg, Berlin, Amsterdam, The Hague, Rotterdam, Brussels and Paris. As well as some other Finnish works the programme included the First Symphony, the *Kalevala* legends, *The Swan of Tuonela* and *Lemminkäinen's home-coming*, *Finlandia*, and the *King Christian II* suite. The leading critics of Europe now had the opportunity to become acquainted with all these works, and this, for Sibelius, was of the utmost significance.

It was no less important that in the summer of 1901 he had the opportunity to perform the two *Kalevala* legends with the Music Society that had been founded in Heidelberg by Liszt and now, as the Universal German Musical Association, was directed by Richard Strauss. The concerts of this Association were widely known and attended by connoisseurs of music from many countries. The *Legends* of the Finnish composer aroused much interest among them and in general were hailed as significant and new.

Sibelius spent the whole winter abroad before this important performance in Heidelberg, with his wife and his two small daughters; first in Berlin and afterwards in Rapallo, Italy. While the family stayed in a *pension* by the sea Sibelius rented a room in the mountains so that he could work undisturbed.

Here, in the Italian spring, the first sketches for the Second Symphony—which is among his most popular works—had their origin. To some extent this work and the First Symphony made an independent group. The composer's emotions are once more anchored in Romanticism, but the feeling of *Sturm und Drang* begins to diminish, and Sibelius is now entirely himself. One is no longer conscious of Tchaikovsky. There is also to be noticed in the D major Symphony a striving for greater concentration and clarity. This tendency is also apparent in the revision of *En Saga* which came later in the same year. For the rest the Second Symphony, like the First, is powerful and dramatic. It has been said of the heroic, climactic finale that it is among the most effective movements in symphonic literature. Various writers, no doubt influenced by each other, have contended that herein Sibelius wished to refer to the successful outcome of the Finnish struggle for freedom. Sibelius himself, however, categorically denied this.

The need for tranquillity in which to work, and love of nature, moved the composer in 1904 to settle in the country. In Järvenpää, some four miles from Helsinki, he had built a house for himself— the villa Ainola—which from now on was to be his permanent home.

In this year a new epoch commenced for Sibelius, not only in respect of things in general but also of his creative life. In the Third Symphony, the first of the greater works that came into being in Ainola, the striving for simplification is completely realized. The emotional, 'pathetic', strain has disappeared; the thematic material is straightforward; wind instruments and percussion are held back; and strings dominate. Sibelius has left his Romantic period behind him and the work is in general to be regarded as transitional. This, however, is hardly sufficient to indicate why this is among the least often played symphonies of Sibelius. The complete simplicity of the restrained beauty of the second movement *Andantino con moto, quasi allegretto* never fails to make an impression. There is something of a similarity, albeit remote, to the *Allegretto* of Brahms's Third Symphony, but Sibelius's principal theme is more original than that of Brahms.

The music of the Finnish master gradually became better and better known abroad. His reputation spread from Heidelberg—at first principally in the west. Very soon there were performances of the major works in England and the U.S.A., and in December 1905 Sibelius himself conducted in England for the first time. He paid further visits in 1908 and 1912, and in general he enjoyed much success in a number of countries which performed his music.

Nevertheless, these years of increasing fame cannot be described as entirely fortunate, for Sibelius's health was at that time giving cause for serious concern. He had a tumour in the throat, and the doctors were afraid of cancer. A tedious course of treatment in Finland was unavailing and after an unsuccessful operation at the beginning of 1908 Sibelius sought the assistance of a specialist in Berlin. After thirteen futile and painful operations the doctors were finally able to remove the tumour. But the risk of cancer remained for many years.

This 'frightening warning from above' as Sibelius referred to it could not but have influence on the works that appeared in those years. The Fourth Symphony and the String Quartet *Voces intimae* are characterized by deep seriousness, and both works are among Sibelius's most significant.

The String Quartet is unique in this output. It is true that in early youth he had written a lot of chamber music, but he had no regard for this later on. The B flat major quartet of 1889 is the only piece (of that period) with an opus number, but it is unpublished and almost never played. *Voces intimae*, on the other hand, is of considerable importance and can at any time be compared with the string quartets of the great masters of this genre.

The main work of this period, the Fourth Symphony, is the most contentious composition of Sibelius, which is not to be wondered at. After all that has happened in the field of modern music, the A minor Symphony, with its fine tonal sense, is not likely today to cause any difficulty of understanding to a genuine music-lover. But in April 1911, when the first performance took place in Helsinki, it sounded as though it came from a distant, and strange, world. To the last degree modern and individual, and born half a century before its time, the symphony was bound to arouse astonishment and indignation. No one had written such a work, not even Sibelius himself. Everything in it is simple and economical; it is almost ascetic. In respect of this work it can truly be said that the composer has renounced every means of presenting his message in the most favourable light, to quote Furtwängler's words on Beethoven. The thematic material is terse, laid out in fragments which dissolve into thin air before the listener has a clear idea of what they are. The instrumentation is exceptionally economical, in places almost as in chamber music. The meditative, almost melancholy, character of the music is almost unvaried.

Even today the Fourth Symphony is unintelligible to many, but, on the other hand, it appears to those who are knowledgeable as the composer's most profound utterance. It is often performed and always seems to win new friends.

In the autumn of 1912 Sibelius conducted performances of the A minor Symphony at the Birmingham Festival and in several other towns in England, and at the beginning of the next year it had its New York *première*. Walter Damrosch was the conductor and thought it a good idea to introduce the symphony to the audience with a few explanatory words. But this did not prevent people from leaving the hall after each movement.

At that time the name of the Finnish composer was already well known in the U.S.A. The real break-through on the other side of the Atlantic had come at the beginning of 1907 with the first performance of the First Symphony in Boston, after which all the main works were several times performed. In the summer of 1914 Sibelius, having accepted an invitation to do so, made an American tour that can be described almost as a triumphal progress.

The Music Festival at Norfolk (Virginia), to which he was invited, was one of the most important annual events in the American musical calendar. The body responsible for the organization of the Festival was the Litchfield County Choral Union, which had been founded by Carl Stoeckel, a millionaire many times over, and an idealist, of Austrian descent.

There was nothing commercial about the Festival, and those

who attended—the *élite* of the American musical world—did so by invitation. In all they numbered some 8,000. The orchestra comprised seventy-five first-class players, whose instruments were of the noblest quality. In his last years Sibelius still spoke enthusiastically of this marvellous orchestra. Each year a famous composer was invited to conduct a work of his own especially written for the Festival as well as other of his compositions. He was given a princely fee, but in spite of this the new work remained his property. Among others who had conducted at Norfolk before Sibelius were Antonin Dvořák, Camille Saint-Saëns and Max Bruch. Every wish of the guest was promptly fulfilled. He determined the times and frequency of rehearsal, the constitution of the orchestra and everything else besides. He lived like a nobleman, or, more properly, like an American multi-millionaire, for whom only the best is good enough.

After the Music Festival Sibelius and Stoeckel made several excursions in Stoeckel's luxurious motor-car or by rail in his private Pullman coach. Among the places visited were the Niagara Falls, which Sibelius had particularly wished to see. At the end of his visit and shortly before his departure in mid-June Sibelius was given an honorary Doctorate at Yale University. At the degree ceremony the music consisted entirely of works by Sibelius.

Stimulated by his considerable success, Sibelius had outlined many bold plans for the future. But scarcely had he returned to Europe before the outbreak of the First World War brought everything to nought. Finland was cut off from the rest of the world, and for four long years Sibelius was unable any more to perform his works abroad just when it would have been most important for him.

All the more enthusiastically then was he honoured in his own land when in December 1915 he celebrated his fiftieth birthday. For this day Sibelius had written his Fifth Symphony, which later he twice revised. At the Festival Concert, in which the tone poem *The Oceanides* composed for Norfolk was given its first performance in Finland, it was welcomed with fanfares and massive applause.

In his Fifth Symphony Sibelius had forsaken the brooding

character of the Fourth. It is a true festival symphony, full of life and brilliance, with its immense finale symbolizing the high peak of the career of its creator. Right from the start this symphony took its place among the most frequently performed of the master's works. He always used to like to talk about this symphony, which for him was so bound up with happy memories. He also never forgot a phenomenon of nature he experienced just when he had put his pen to this score for the last time. Twelve white swans settled down on the lake, and then circled his home three times before flying away.

There now followed a seven-year period which brought forth numerous violin and piano pieces, as well as some for voices, but no new major orchestral works. The first such work which followed the period was the Sixth Symphony, a glorious work of classical grandeur that like the Third Symphony is, however, very seldom played. Sibelius himself has correctly said that it is somehow uncongenial to our age.

The Seventh Symphony is a complete contrast to the Sixth—although it was only one year later that its first performance took place in Stockholm—and has become very popular. This work has provided especial interest for musical scholars since it was written without division into movements. In spite of this there is hardly any other symphony that is more perfect. The American critic Olin Downes wrote:

> Here a form was attained through which the flow of the composer's ideas were set free rather than confined. There are no words to describe this freedom, this powerful unity, this absolute consistency, this irresistible mastery.

The last two symphonies to a certain extent are twins. They appeared practically at the same time as the result of a longer process of creation, and they are closely related in respect of their general character. The serene majesty of the Sixth Symphony also dominates the Seventh.

The last important work of Sibelius was the tone poem *Tapiola* which he wrote in 1926, after he had composed the incidental music for Shakespeare's *The Tempest*, as a commission for the Royal Theatre in Copenhagen just before his sixtieth birthday.

This contained thirty-four pieces, of which Sibelius selected seventeen for concert use.

From the fourteen sets of incidental music by Sibelius the last named and the music for Maurice Maeterlinck's *Pelléas et Mélisande* are to be regarded as most important. The suite from *King Christian II* is very popular. The remaining works of this kind are less frequently performed, except for the world-famed *Valse triste*, which was composed for *Kuolema*, a tragedy by Arvid Järnefelt, the composer's brother-in-law.

Sibelius almost without exception spent his long old age in Järvenpää. It was seldom that he visited the capital, and his last public appearance was at the Festival Concert in celebration of his seventieth birthday, in December 1935, but he did not himself conduct.

He died on 20th September 1957, almost ninety-two years of age.

ONE

⤷⤷

The first meeting

One of the five sons-in-law of Jean Sibelius was Deputy General
Director of the largest Finnish commercial bank in which I too
had worked for many years. One day he asked me if I felt inclined
to look after the correspondence of the famous composer as a part-
time job. I had the right qualifications, for my profession entailed
translating from and writing letters in foreign languages, and I had
also already to a small extent tried my hand at literature. Moreover,
I came from a musical family and played the violin.

If during Sibelius's lifetime in Finland one were asked if one
were prepared to do anything for the great composer there was, as
a rule, only one possible answer. In his native land Sibelius had a
place allowed to few other men. As the leading Finnish artist he had
achieved real fame relatively early. He was the voice of Finland
in the world, and this voice was of great significance for his people.

When Sibelius made his break-through with the symphonic
work *Kullervo* at the beginning of 1892 Finland was an autono-
mous state under Russian rule. But the autonomy of Finland was
a thorn in the flesh so far as the Czar—or rather, his advisers—was
concerned, for he himself was hardly more than a cipher. Finland
was to be but 'a plot of Russian territory', as a conservative
Russian newspaper put it, and no more. In consequence of this,
laws and injunctions were promulgated in contradiction of
Finnish autonomy, while otherwise Finnish laws were violated or
abrogated without scruple.

The Finns had not the slightest intention of allowing themselves to be subjugated. Newspapers were withdrawn, organizations forbidden, and officials prosecuted; but none of this helped

the Russians at all. The anti-Russian attitudes grew from year to year, and the people formed a strong national front. In culture Finland felt herself to stand at a far remove from Russia, which boasted more illiteracy than practically any other country in Europe.

What chance had a small nation of about three million of defending itself against the Russian giant? Art, science, and social progress in this little country alone could show the civilized world that the Finns had the right to maintain their independence as one of the cultural nations of Europe. All achievements in the province of culture were vital to the fatherland. They were the inner power of the so-called passive resistance that inspired the whole people.

These were the political conditions under which Jean Sibelius spent his youth, and they had decisive significance for him. On the one hand he was himself permeated with the spirit of nationalism, which could not but exert influence on his creative work; on the other he was carried along by the flow of patriotism, which afforded him a point of departure available to few young artists. The Finns could have wished at that exact point in time for nothing more than an artist who had something vital to say, and who spoke an international language.

So it was that already in his youth Sibelius gained a wholly extraordinary popularity in his native land. His compositions were widely interpreted more or less as battle songs and as representing the general mood of the Finnish people. Most especially was this so in respect of the tone poem *Finlandia*, which was very quickly recognized both abroad and at home as a second national anthem. In concerts of Sibelius's music the voice of the fatherland was ever to be heard, and he was honoured as Finland's most famous son.

Sibelius held this high place for the whole of his life, and the more his fame grew in the world the more affection and esteem there were for him in his own country. In independent Finland Sibelius was practically a legendary figure, one of the elect, to be approached only with reverence.

This then was the man for whom I was now to work, but

hitherto had never seen. For years he had lived in his villa, Ainola, in Järvenpää without ever making a public appearance. But there were pictures of him everywhere, and now I took an especially good look at them. The impression was not exactly encouraging. An energetic mouth and a much-wrinkled forehead suggested a powerful and somewhat unemotional man. I jumped to the conclusion that he was old, easily irritated, and incapable of appreciating a joke. Somewhat intimidated I paid my first visit to him.

How surprised I was when for the first time I was face to face with the famous composer in the largest room in Ainola. An impressive, robust man approached with firm steps, his whole being seeming to radiate cordiality and warmth of feeling. The friendly expression of his face was such that the severity of the four- or five-fold wrinkles of his forehead disappeared. Under the bushy eyebrows two bright grey eyes shone out, their expression changing all the time. The sharp look seemed as though it pierced into the depths of my soul. In a flash he understood that his secretary-to-be was terrified, and made a light-hearted remark that promptly brightened the atmosphere. Sibelius possessed the rare gift of always being able to find the right word for any occasion.

His voice was deep and masculine, and I reflected quickly that it must also be a good singing voice. But then I remembered what the friend of his youth, the writer Adolf Paul, had once said: 'By God! He was never a singer; but he made beautiful songs.'

At the time Sibelius was seventy-two, but didn't look it. He moved more like a man of fifty, and he was pretty vigorous. The blond artist's locks of his youth, which always looked black in photographs of those days, had completely vanished. For years the prominent head of the master—with the high, wrinkled, brow —had been bald. The ears were unusually large and beautifully formed. It could scarcely have been fortuitous that it was indeed a great musician who had such ears.

I would like to draw especial attention to the master's eyes, for they were so uncommonly expressive. I have never known any other man in whose eyes there was so much play of emotion. The basic quality was a warm friendliness, of the sort that one does not often encounter in men. On this permanent foundation, so to speak, an astonishingly rich range of colours glowed. Sometimes the master's gaze surprisingly dimmed, and seemed almost without life. But in the next moment there was a cheerful, almost boyish, twinkle, and suddenly, quite without reason—for he had only said the most cordial things—Sibelius looked at me with the razor-keen eyes of a falcon, as though he would bore right into my soul. He himself said that he could subdue a lion with a look, and I believed he could.

His glance could also reflect the deepest sorrow, as if all the misery of his whole life could have been concentrated into a single moment. But that never lasted long. In a moment I was, maybe, privileged to see the most beautiful expression of which the human glance is capable. When Sibelius was excited by something—a melody, a few words, an idea—his eyes suddenly opened wide and shone with the whole glow of his artist's soul. I have never forgotten that look. It mirrored a strength of feeling and warmth of heart that are to be found in very few men.

This warmth was accorded to me in rich measure right from our first meeting. A powerful man of the rank, more or less, of managing director, wanted to question me as to my competence and said, 'Fine! Now we will at once decide what you will have to do for me, and how I will have the correspondence dealt with.' But that was not the way of Sibelius. For him purely human values always claimed first place. About his own wishes he had never a word to say. Instead, he began to talk about me in the most friendly manner, asking if my parents were still alive, if I had children, what I was interested in as well as my work, and so on. When he learned that I had written a few books, he remarked with amusing contrition that he had never read them—as though this was a severe loss to him. All in all he treated me not as a member of his staff, but as an esteemed guest.

After a while he asked me if I would like to eat lunch. I almost took fright over this surprising question. How could I have anticipated—hardly having entered the house—that I might be sitting at the luncheon table with the great man? Without considering the matter for long I courteously declined the invitation saying—what was also true—that I had already eaten. Subsequently I kicked myself for being so stupid, for in due course it became clear that Sibelius had waited lunch for me, although it was fairly late in the afternoon when I came to Ainola. Our managing director would have said at this point: 'Ah well! Now I'll have a quick bite of food. In the meantime you can attend to the correspondence.' But Sibelius was much too civilized for that sort of thing. So it happened that on account of his new secretary the master had to start the relationship by going hungry.

I was, however, able to take a little comfort. After we had drunk coffee he smoked a cigar—indeed he smoked two cigars—although as a non-smoker I for my part had refused the thick Havana he offered me.

When at last we spoke of my work everything turned out quite differently from what I expected. I waited in vain for requests and instructions. Sibelius briefly explained what it was all about and then asked me to decide for myself how the work should be carried out. Several times he let me know how grateful he was that I had stated my readiness to help him.

'When there is an important letter to be answered,' he said with a roguish glint in his grey eyes, 'we have almost the whole family worried.'

After that he told me this and that about his previous secretaries. They had all only been with him for short periods. One elegant young woman was so worked up at her first visit that she promptly smashed the typewriter.

'She played a passage of Liszt on the keys, and that's how it happened,' said Sibelius as he described a mighty arpeggio in the air with both hands. 'We—the whole family—stood there in amazement and looked on the destruction.'

The typewriter was sent to be repaired, and the first visit of that young lady was her last. Mrs Sibelius and the daughters had to deal with the correspondence again.

I made a mess of many things during the long years in which I worked for Sibelius. I did not destroy any typewriters, but for the rest every conceivable mistake and oversight had its certain place in those twenty years. But I never heard a cross word on account of

them. Kind and considerate, as on that first day, out of the sheer
goodness of his heart Sibelius put up with all my inadequacies
through the long years. 'That was at the time,' he once said to me,
'when the dear God sent you to us.' That was right, except that
the dear God had not given consideration to him but to me. And
for that I am grateful to Him for the rest of my life.

TWO

▷▷

Ainola

Ainola, where for years now I was to come and go, stands on a wooded hill, about 200 yards from the main road. The foundation stone of the house was laid at the beginning of 1904 and in the following autumn the family moved into their new home. The composer was thirty-eight at the time, and felt that his work needed a quiet environment. Another reason for his early retirement to the country was certainly his love of nature. Järvenpää in many ways was a suitable place for a creative artist to live. It was near the capital, Helsinki, which could be reached either by rail or road in about an hour, and it was at that time a haven of peace and quiet. Other well-known artists had also retreated to Järvenpää. The painters Pekka Halonen and Eero Järnefelt, Sibelius's brother-in-law, lived there. So too did Juhani Aho who, at the turn of the century, was the most important writer in Finland.

Ainola is a two-storied wooden house, of which the outside walls are of white-painted boards. It stands on a slope that faces south and is easily visible from the main road. In front of the house there are magnificent pine-trees growing. In the course of years they hid the view more and more, but Sibelius would never be parted from them. Everything was to remain in its natural state. The estate, several times enlarged through acquisition, and some nine acres in extent, is almost entirely wooded.

A small track through the woods leads from the entrance up to the villa. It is just wide enough to allow a motor-car to draw up at the steps at the entrance. One parked one's car on a small, level patch of ground in front of the villa, where there are some beautiful birches, which throw their shadow over the window of the guest-room on the upper floor. It was at this window that Sibelius composed his Seventh and last Symphony.

The entrance to the villa is on the north side. Visitors first crossed a big, open veranda, where a table and several chairs stood in the summer. When the weather allowed, it was usual for Sibelius to bid farewell to his guests on the veranda. From there during his long life he waved goodbye to hundreds of people. Many was the time I also stood there having a parting few words with the master before getting into my car.

There was always a great deal of light and sun on the ground floor of Ainola, because practically all the windows faced south. The impression of spaciousness was strengthened because the drawing-room and dining-room were not divided by a solid wall. Sibelius had had the original opening for a door much enlarged. Until then the drawing-room had served as the composer's work-room. The Third Symphony, the tone-poems *Pohjola's Daughter* and *Night-ride and Sunrise*, the string quartet *Voces intimae*, the incidental music for August Strindberg's *Swanwhite*, and a considerable number of smaller works were written, and the Violin Concerto revised, here.

A third room on the ground floor, to which guests had access, was the so-called library on the south of the villa. When I was there this was used as a living-room. Next to this at that time were the master's workroom and bedroom, and then, finally, the kitchen.

In designing the interiors the architect had taken the Finnish 'cottage style' as his model. The beams in the ceiling were all left uncovered and appropriately darkened. The general impression this created was magnificent and it was heightened in the dining-room by a large green fireplace. Except for the drawing-room, where there was wallpaper, all the rooms had their natural wood-walls.

The upper floor was extended for the first time in 1911. Sibelius then chose as his study a small, sparsely furnished room over the drawing-room, with a beautiful view across the fields to Tuusula Lake. The first great work composed in this room—the austere Fourth Symphony—expressed its puritanical character.

Also on the upper floor there was a large room which was first used as a bedroom but later served the mistress of the house for her own domestic pursuits. The whole upper floor had a feeling of warm comfort such, for example, as used to be found in manor houses in times past.

Downstairs I could go anywhere blindfold, and I knew the interior decorations in the last years almost as well as those of my own home. They testified above all to an old culture and had their own quality of refinement. The furniture, without exception in good taste though in no sense luxurious, was in the style of the first two decades of the century. Only the library had modern appointments. The large grey armchairs and a low, wide, table with a glass top contrasted with the grand style of the house. I carried out my duties on this table whenever I dealt with the post. Sibelius almost always sat opposite to me and Mrs Sibelius was also frequently there.

The composer himself thought his home was very modest and often spoke humorously on the subject. 'The Americans,' he said, 'are accustomed to the idea that famous men live like lords. They expect to find a castle here, and are very disappointed when they see our little house.'

Ainola was no castle, but it contained more things of importance in the history of culture than a good many Americans could imagine. They had gradually accumulated during the composer's long life. Almost all the well-known Finnish artists were represented by works, of which most bore dedicatory inscriptions in the artists' hands. Many things directly connected with the master's celebrated career caught one's attention. For instance, there were the only two laurel wreaths which could find places on the wall. These—in the library—were magnificent, and had been given to the great composer in the name of the Finnish people.

A vast number of gifts of different kinds had been collected over the years. Among them was the large Steinway grand in the drawing-room, which Sibelius received on the occasion of his fiftieth birthday. In a corner of the same room was a tall cupboard with glass doors in which Addresses, Diplomas and Plaquettes were kept. Sibelius had acquired honorary membership of so many bodies that it was impossible for him to remember them all. I often heard him asking himself, 'Should I be an honorary member of this Association?' He was also honorary Doctor and honorary Professor of a number of universities. Two large caskets hardly sufficed to hold all his orders and medals, among which several were very rare.

In the years in which I went to Ainola the neighbourhood was still very isolated. There were almost no near neighbours, but on that account there were the more four-legged inhabitants of the woods. An Italian admirer once sent a poem, in which he had intended, in a vast number of stanzas, to describe how the great musician in his solitude lived with the wild animals. He counted up everything from squirrel and stoat to stag, and the list included many animals that were never to be found in Finland. In the early part of the year, however, mountain-hens and moorhens were frequent visitors to the garden, and perhaps a stately stag with his mighty antlers would appear before the window to the master's great delight—not to speak of hares and foxes.

Although Sibelius and his family lived so much apart it never entered anybody's head to worry about their safety. In earlier times—alas, only in earlier times—the Finns were known for their absolute honesty and reliability. Until the 1950s one lived in Ainola in a state of almost childlike trust and idyllic calm. The last of the dogs had been dead for years and, especially in summer, the outer doors remained open even at night. In former times this was customary in Finland. But at the end of 1952 it was otherwise. In the night before Christmas Eve the master's house was honoured by a visit from a burglar. As always Sibelius was late in going to bed and could remember that he only got to sleep at four o'clock in the morning. When he awoke at seven he immediately noticed that the drawer of his writing-table was open and some 60,000 Marks (then worth 750 German Marks) had vanished.

The police in Järvenpää were immediately notified and it was soon established that the intruder was a murderer who had escaped from prison in the neighbourhood of Järvenpää. It was child's play for an experienced burglar to break into the villa, for the kitchen-door had a very primitive lock, and as a rule perhaps, it was left undone. The man went from the kitchen into the dining-room and from there he reached the composer's workroom and bedroom. There, in absolute silence, he had stolen all the money while Sibelius slept a few steps away from him. On leaving the house he had taken a swig out of the cream can, gulped down some groats and stuffed a box of caviare into his case. Everything pointed to his having been loitering near the house for some nights and thereby getting himself well orientated.

Sibelius was indignant. His grey eyes struck fire when he told me what had taken place. He took the break-in almost as a personal insult. 'My first idea,' he said gloomily, 'was to leave Finland for ever. It was lucky that I did not wake up. Such impudence would have made me very angry—and the man would have killed me for sure.'

Henceforth all the outside doors of Ainola were fitted with first-class locks and the low window of the ante-room with whitened iron bars. The police refused to give any information about the burglary for publication. It would have caused a big sensation, and the telephone-lines from Ainola to buzz for days. The foreign, especially the American, press would have printed headlines giving an entire false impression of conditions in Finland.

THREE

⊳⊳⊳

Life companion

Almost every great composer has had an understanding woman near to him, to understand him, to urge him to the greatest endeavour. Perhaps this was especially so in the case of the Romantics. George Sand was the inspiration of Frédéric Chopin, and Clara Schumann of her husband and of Brahms. Wagner had Mathilde von Wesendonck and Cosima Liszt—whom he appropriated from Hans von Bülow.

Sibelius had Aino Järnefelt, his wife and his only great love. She was the daughter of a general, and her mother was of the family of Clodt von Jurgensburg. She was twenty when she married the young composer in June 1892, a few months after he had become famous as a result of the *Kullervo* Symphony. Sibelius and Aino had already been engaged for a year or two, and it is tempting to think that young love had played a part—even, perhaps, a decisive part—in the creation of this work. Very soon after their marriage Sibelius composed his second important work, *En Saga*.

Sibelius said to me on a number of occasions that without his wife he would never have been able to execute his life's work. What he meant by that he never defined more precisely, but anyone who knew the close spiritual communion which united those two all through their life together appreciates that it was not only a matter of help in externals, although this too was always needed by Sibelius. Aino Sibelius came from an artistic family. Baroness Clodt von Jurgensburg had a considerable appreciation of art and all her three sons were artists. Arvid Järnefelt was one of the best Finnish writers of his time, and Eero one of the best painters. The youngest son, Armas, was a musician and ended his career as

Court Music Director in Stockholm. Aino, then, before her marriage had learned at home how to appreciate the needs of an artist, and Sibelius often used to remark on this. That she was musical goes without saying: when she was young she had a good knowledge of the literature of music, and played the piano very well.

But a woman whose destiny was to inspire a great artist needed much more. It is not every loving woman who can reach so far, for it takes a personality with important innate qualities. During the long time I worked for Sibelius I had plenty of opportunity to get to know his life's companion. What I always admired was the rare sincerity and honesty which she applied to all she undertook. She was quite incapable of untruth, even indirectly or passively. I believe that it was exactly this purity of thought and feeling that enabled her to be a support to the master. It was only thus that she could raise herself to that spiritual level on which the great musician moved.

At the same time I certainly would not have said that Aino Sibelius had a direct share in her husband's work as a composer. It could have happened that Sibelius went to the piano, played two chords, and asked his wife which was the better, but in the end he always chose the one that pleased him more. It was the same with Brahms, who often sought but rarely took Clara Schumann's advice in respect of new works. Aino always assured me that she never participated in her husband's work in any shape or form.

She was, therefore, able to offer stronger spiritual support. Seldom has any woman encompassed the works of her husband with such affection as Aino Sibelius. She knew every bar of the symphonies from memory. From the very moment of their conception they were a source of joy for her. Once she described her feelings to me almost dramatically:

> How many nights have I lain awake in my bed and listened to my husband writing in the next room! A great orchestral work takes a long time to mature in his mind. For days I can perceive the creative process taking place, and I remain quite silent so as not to disturb him. In the night he moves about restlessly in his room. From time to time he sits down at his writing-desk, and then once again paces to and fro. I can't sleep, and in the

silence of my room I am alone and yet with him during those difficult hours. The work is not yet matured. I know this exactly, and night after night with anxious heart I wait on the great, final outcome. Then eventually one night the moment comes. As so often before, I hear him seat himself at his desk and then all at once he begins to draw the bar-lines. My husband never writes the parts one by one, but composes for all the instruments simultaneously. The whole score develops bar by bar. When the writing down begins, he works very quickly. Through the closed door I hear the rub of the pen as he draws long bar-lines across the whole page. It is a great event for me too. A heavy load falls from my heart. At such a time I am deeply happy.

When Sibelius celebrated his seventieth birthday and received a tremendous number of testimonies of respect, his wife said in an interview to a woman journalist:

His work is my one and only concern. I have felt myself fortunate to be with him. I certainly won't say that it has always been easy. To a certain extent I have had to restrain and keep a bridle on myself. But my destiny was as a blessing and a gift from above. My husband's music is like the Word of God. It comes from a noble source and it is fine to live close by it.

It had certainly not been easy for her. She bore the weight of everyday things while her husband was busy with his creative work, or while he was away. Like so many artists Sibelius was awkward and clumsy in practical matters, in fact, as helpless as a child. He could hardly knock a nail in the wall. He needed someone, preferably a woman, to take charge of his affairs. Providentially Sibelius was surrounded all his life by helpful women. He was brought up by his mother, two grandmothers, and two aunts. Aino gave him five daughters but not one son. In his later years from time to time he had eight women about the house, for there were also the two maids who worked for years at Ainola and almost belonged to the family.

I asked Sibelius half in jest if he would not have liked to have had a son.

'Oh no! I have never in fact thought about it,' he answered quite spontaneously. 'My daughters became so dear to me and I have had so much pleasure from them that I could not have wanted for anything better.'

Mrs Sibelius was sitting by us and quietly added: 'For my part I needed no other son than my husband.'

Without doubt she had hit the nail on the head. In earlier years especially Sibelius could be as thoughtless as a child. This thoughtlessness and his frequently astonishing notions often made life difficult for his wife and children. He freely admitted this, saying:

An artist shouldn't have a family, for the woman always suffers. I have lived very thoughtlessly, and that was wrong of me. A man on his own can order his life as he wishes, but the father of a family can't do what I've done all my life. We would have succumbed to our difficulties if I had not had a wife who always looked after everything and worked like a slave, so that we should keep our heads above water.

Nor had Aino Sibelius shied from bodily 'slave work'. The garden at Ainola today covers a wide expanse. In addition to magnificent flowers, each summer brings forth vegetables and fruit-bushes of every kind. But it was not always so. When Ainola was built more than sixty years ago, where the present garden is there was no more than a wilderness of stone. To put a kitchen garden there was a huge task and at the start the young woman had to do everything herself. 'I hacked and shovelled away every day,' she told me. 'In between whiles I complained bitterly and then went on shovelling.'

At the beginning there were a few small beds, but gradually they increased. Soil was procured and labour brought in from outside. In later years the garden provided the family with fruit, berries and vegetables the whole year through. Even today I think sadly on the delicate bottled peas and beans which I used to eat at Ainola in mid-winter. In the autumn, when everything was ripe, the daughters came and went back to their families in town with full baskets.

They had a lot to be grateful to their mother for, and they appreciated it to the full. There was a warm, intimate, link between Aino Sibelius and her children. She had even given lessons to her five daughters because there was no money for their education, and they were all so well prepared that they went only through the top classes in school, and the entrance examination of the two youngest girls was hardly regarded more seriously than as an unimportant formality.

They were gifted, and very beautiful, daughters that Aino Sibelius had given to her husband. They not only gave him great pleasure, as he said, but in many ways were able to help him. A man like Sibelius, especially in his later years, needed many representatives, and his daughters were, so to speak, made for the job. He assigned duties of widely varying kinds to them, and on a number of occasions they represented him in other countries. He was very grateful to them. To his daughters, as to his wife, Sibelius was always cavalier. Many times in the course of his life he caused them trouble through his thoughtlessness, but he always recompensed them through his goodness of heart.

A woman could scarcely have wished for a kinder husband. He expressed his appreciation in warm terms, and often excused himself to her when, in my prosaic view, there was no occasion so to do. 'I haven't made you sad, dear Aino?' This was a question I often heard, sometimes surprisingly. Sibelius offered little courtesies to his wife as a matter of course. 'How nice that you've come nearer,' he could say all of a sudden, if she changed her chair. If she were ill in her bedroom on the first floor one could be sure that she was always in his thoughts. In later years an internal telephone was installed, and then Sibelius would call his wife simply to say that he felt lonely without her.

To strangers he always stressed how much he had to thank her for. 'How great has been my fortune in having been able to live with her all the long years,' he said to me, with force, more than once.

One day the conversation turned to a period of eight years during which the doctor had forbidden him to smoke.

'Nothing else was disturbing at that time,' said Mrs Sibelius. 'Those were the happiest years of my life.'

'What!' cried Sibelius, 'You were only granted eight years. And I have been happy with you all my life.'

When Aino Sibelius was seventy-five years old the master delivered such a beautiful after-dinner speech that most of the guests had tears in their eyes. 'You, perhaps, might have been happier with someone else,' he said, 'but I, never.' Ten years later, when he was more than ninety, he climbed up the steep staircase early on the morning of his wife's birthday, although forbidden to do so by the doctor. He carried a huge bunch of roses to give to his wife, as at the beginning of their life together. He said: 'I come now to court for a second time.'

And, as so many times before, Aino Sibelius assured him that she had never repented of her first answer.

FOUR

⊳⊳

Sibelius the man

To give a clear picture of Jean Sibelius is no easy task. That he was a genius does not need emphasizing. The celebrated Finnish mathematician Rolf Nevelinna, Member of the Finnish Academy, once said that he had known many famous men in science and the arts—Paul Hindemith was one of them—but in none had genius been so apparent as in Sibelius.

I believe, however, although I have only known one man of real greatness, that all genius must have something of a general quality, an inborn versatility and spiritual superiority, which one meets only in such men. Men of talent, distinguished specialists, are often limited and uninteresting. They know their own field through and through but only there can they claim superiority. A man of genius on the other hand approaches all aspects of life from a higher plane and comprehends things strange to him with almost superhuman understanding that one would hardly have credited him with. To a certain degree he has a sixth sense, and it is this sixth sense that distinguishes genius from talent and enables it to scale the highest peaks. A man of genius is generally a fascinating personality, because of his profound understanding of his fellowmen.

I can vouch for all of that in respect of Sibelius, and I hope to be able to communicate my impression of him. Little would be achieved by theoretical discussion, and so I believe that I shall best serve my purpose by simply relating what I heard and saw in the course of years at Ainola.

Very early on I began to collect material and to make notes of anything that seemed important and interesting. At first I was disinclined to tell the master, for I knew that he did not at all like his private life to be publicized. But to be able to hide anything from his falcon's eyes was a vain hope. I frequently made notes of key phrases at Ainola, and very soon he observed it. In any case he could easily guess that I would write about him, and one day he said: 'I have seen that you are taking notes. I can well understand that, but I would like to ask you not to publish anything about me before my death.'

After we had come to an agreement about this I no longer needed to avoid the subject. On the contary, Sibelius told me many different things about his life and his work. In later years after I had published a comprehensive biography of Robert and Clara Schumann, he even made small notes for me. These mostly concerned wrong information about him which was in circulation and which I was to put right in my book. Sometimes he even wrote a more extended list of comments. He used to make me sit at the table while he turned this way and that as he related his story.

It was not always easy to get information from him, however. Certain questions he avoided consistently. Every man wishes his life and character to be shown according to his own point of view, and to a direct question I did not always get a direct answer.

Besides, Sibelius had an unusually lively—I might almost say restless—temperament. His movements were quick and his ideas were continually changing. He would rarely sit for long in the same chair. Suddenly he would jump up and quickly get a cigar before anyone had time to help him. Exhaustive discussion of one question was not for him, for his imagination continually made associations which took his thoughts in new directions. In the middle of a conversation something would come into his mind, and at once he would change the subject. Humour was a funda-mental trait in his character, and he could see the funny side of most things. His speech was spiced with humorous turns of phrase and flashes of wit.

It was a hot July day in 1938 when I came to Ainola for the first time. Sibelius was seventy-two, and behind him lay a long life which had finally formed his character and bearing. The two further decades that were allotted to him surely matured the inner man even though his outward appearance did not change much.

In the course of years he became more dignified. The pale youngster with indifferent health, on account of which he had to pay an increased insurance premium in 1889, had developed into a patriarch, whose robust form and proud bearing always drew attention to him. He appeared to tower over everybody physically. It was only after some time that I realized that he was a centimetre or two shorter than I was myself—178 cm. to be precise.

He remained dignified and patriarchal to the end. The old master's vigour and physical condition gave rise to much wonderment, he was never an old man in the accepted sense of that term. Every day he smoked several large cigars and ate everything with a good appetite. 'I have always lived an unhealthy life,' he said. When he was eighty-seven I noticed for the first time that he did not any more have a small brandy at lunch. A letter in which he was questioned about the influence of tobacco and alcohol on his work went unanswered, but he said to me: 'All the doctors who wanted to forbid me to smoke and to drink are dead. But I am quietly going on living. It's not every man of my age who can unhesitatingly eat and drink as I do.'

He was obviously proud that he had remained in good condition for so long. It amused him very much when any visitor stood wide-eyed in the doorway, making up his mind if the robust and elegant gentleman who approached him with firm steps could in fact be the old Jean Sibelius. He was also a good actor, and always knew how to hide lassitude and listlessness from his guests.

In the autumn of 1950, when Sibelius was eighty-five, a tooth that had been hurting him for a long time had to be extracted. The dentist was worried, fearing that the old man could die of shock. In the end he said he was prepared to operate but refused all responsibility. Everything went smoothly and Sibelius went home in the best of moods. Before the nerve was anaesthetized the dentist had offered him a glass of brandy. 'He seemed somewhat surprised when I quickly downed the cognac,' said Sibelius with a pleased grin. 'Not every octogenarian takes after me.'

A few days before his eightieth birthday I had to carry a heavy box from Ainola to the main road. Sibelius came with me into the ante-room, and, courteous as ever, said he was sorry about this imposition. Suddenly he took the box by the handle, lifted it in the air as though it were empty cardboard, and then gently put it back on the ground. 'It doesn't, after all, seem all that heavy,' he said delightedly. I was of quite another opinion, but I kept it to myself. Right up to the last Sibelius was astonishingly energetic and full of life. He demonstrated this one July evening in 1957, only a month or two before his death. At the same time he gave everyone at Ainola a horrible shock.

We were sitting in the library after work, with a cup of coffee. Besides Sibelius and his wife, their eldest daughter, Mrs Eva Paloheimo, was there. After Sibelius had drunk his coffee he put a chair in front of the radio, sat down, and tried to get some music. As always, he soon lost his enthusiasm and went back to his previous place. After a while, however, he returned to the radio again and began to look for this or that station. But in the meantime someone had put the chair on one side. Sibelius had not noticed, and to my horror I suddenly saw him sit down on thin air. His legs folded up and he fell on his back, and it seemed to me that his head hit the floor—though lightly. Fortunately there was a carpet, if a rather thin one, in the room.

We all leapt up in alarm. Mrs Paloheimo had been sitting near the radio and was the first on the spot. She had already helped her father to his feet when I had rushed over from my place behind the table. We all stood round him with heavy hearts.

And what about Sibelius himself? At first he appeared somewhat astonished, as though he wondered how he had actually got onto the floor. Then, suddenly, the comedy of the situation dawned on him. Like a schoolboy, on whom someone had played a joke, he burst into cheerful laughter. After a while the rest of us felt like laughing too.

An examination afterwards showed that there was nothing amiss. He had obviously had the presence of mind in falling to do so with sufficient agility to avoid knocking himself. A few years before this particular evening Basil Cameron had visited Ainola to discuss the *Lemminkäinen* legends, which he wished to conduct in

London. He explained how at that time it was the fashion among older people to do everything with the least possible expenditure of energy. It was most important of all how one sat down in and got up from one's chair. Cameron described exactly how it should be done, with ease and smoothness. Perhaps it was precisely this out-of-the-way lecture by the famous conductor that had preserved Sibelius from calamity.

Anyway he found the whole affair nothing more than amusing. During the evening he laughed several times about it, finally dissolving into loud peals. 'I must have looked funny sitting on thin air,' he giggled as he puffed a great cloud of cigar smoke.

In his earlier years Sibelius had not taken much care of himself. Later on he suffered from rheumatism, especially during the period when he was doing a lot of conducting abroad. Once on the way to London to conduct performances of his works his right arm became immobile. Luckily he found a man who could help him. This was a Finnish political activist, who lived as a refugee in England, earning his living as a masseur for the wealthy. He injected the arm and as a result Sibelius was able to conduct.

He would, however, take no medicine, but decided that he would steel his body against rheumatism. He preferred sleeping on a simple camp-bed and every morning he had a cold sponge-down—in winter with icy water. The jug stood all night long on the balcony outside the bedroom. In the morning the ice was broken with great care and Sibelius began his treatment.

We once discussed the effect of mental on bodily health. He said:

> I am certain that all my pains and illnesses are of mental origin. The doctors don't believe that, but I know it to be a fact. I knew it even when I was a child. I am also very sensitive to changes of season and weather. The darkest weeks of the year, from my birthday until Christmas, when the sun is at its lowest, are always a difficult time for me. Immediately Christmas is over things improve and life is fun once more.

I myself could often confirm that. If he was tired or under the weather I could be fairly certain that something was pressing on his mind. Depression and worry always affected his physical condition. In the last ten years his hand trembled quite considerably when he was bothered, so much so that he could hardly sign his letters. When on the other hand he was in a sunny mood, he wrote his signature with enthusiasm and elegance. I once mentioned to him that Adolf Paul had said in one of his books that as a student Sibelius had been 'always deathly ill'. 'Indeed,' he said quite spontaneously, 'I had such a rotten violin, you see. Then I got a better one from my grandmother.'

Only a few people knew when he was ill. The old often complain about their troubles, but Sibelius never did. 'Why should I annoy other people with miserable things?' he said. 'Every one of us has sorrows enough of his own. I can't stand it when I hear continued lamentation about a weak heart or rheumatic disorders.' Indeed, sometimes he excused himself to me—his own secretary—for the way in which he expressed his depressions. 'The eighty-year-old machine no longer functions quite efficiently, d'you see.'

Any outside rumour concerning the composer's illnesses we had carefully to prevent. If anything was known about them a mountain was made out of a molehill, for everything relating to the great man's private life immediately made the world press. It could indeed happen that while the master was enjoying the best of health a rumour would get around that he was seriously ill. At once there was a stream of inquiries, telegrams, phone calls. I even got some in Helsinki. Consequently I never let it be known when Sibelius was ill although during our association he had pneumonia three times and it was only his amazing constitution which overcame it.

I particularly remember an evening at the turn of 1945-6 after Sibelius had celebrated his eightieth birthday, which took a good deal out of him. Perhaps the knowledge that his ninth decade had already begun depressed him. When I arrived at Ainola, where every room was full of huge baskets of fragrant flowers, Sibelius received me in bed, something that had never happened before. 'I don't feel at all well,' he said. 'I have been coughing blood, but that's only between the two of us. There's no need for my wife to know, for it would worry her a lot.'

In the meantime Mrs Sibelius and the maid had fetched a large basket with all the birthday and Christmas mail in it, and the three of us began to go through the letters. But very soon it became clear that we couldn't work in the bedroom. Mrs Sibelius and I therefore took a pile of letters each and went with them to the library.

We hadn't been working there for more than a quarter of an hour before Sibelius, who always got dressed very quickly, appeared in the library. To my dismay, instead of asking me to fetch the heavy basket out of the bedroom he brought it himself, as though it were quite light. He had already put it on the table before I was on my feet. Then he sat down in his favourite place in a corner of the library and joined us in our work. After a while he went to the telephone in the dining-room and made a call. We could hear only indistinctly what he said, but Mrs Sibelius remarked: 'He seems to be talking to the doctor. Probably something is worrying him.'

Then we all had lunch together, after which Sibelius went to bed again. Soon afterwards the doctor came and examined his patient. After a while Mrs Sibelius came into the library, where I was still working, and told me, in confidence, that her husband was coughing blood: 'The doctor assures me that his lungs are sound. It is a kind of disturbance of the circulation of the blood, that can occur in extreme old age. But all of this is only between the two of us. He doesn't like people talking about his complaints.'

Sibelius was of the opinion that as regards mental condition a cultured man is more robust than a peasant who had lived under primitive conditions. The need to cultivate the acquaintance of people and to keep to the prescribed conventions, even from childhood, helps to strengthen the will and to develop self-discipline. Sibelius, himself a good actor who was ready for every occasion, was a living example of this thesis. Ruth Snellman, his second daughter and the leading lady of the National Theatre for many years, was right when she said that her father could also have made his name on the stage. Sibelius certainly was often impatient and restless, but when there were visitors, even the most boring, nobody could perceive other than that he was enormously pleased to see them. And in really serious situations he was the most composed of all. He was himself surprised at this.

'When things are serious,' he affirmed, 'I never lose my head.' As an example of 'something serious', Sibelius once told me about a car accident on the way to Helsinki shortly before his seventieth birthday. A horse with a sleigh came out from a side-road and crashed into the car. In trying to avoid it the chauffeur drove into the ditch, but luckily the car stayed on its wheels. The sleigh was shattered, the horse lay bleeding on the road and a crowd of people quickly came clamouring round Sibelius. But he kept perfectly calm, as if nothing out-of-the-way had taken place. This first and, luckily, his last motor-car accident left him practically unmoved.

The Finnish President, P. E. Svinhuvud, who was ill at the time and unable to take part in the festivities, shortly afterwards invited the composer to an audience. He was particularly interested in the car accident and got him to tell him everything that had happened.

In the autumn of 1950 the Danish publisher Asger Wilhelm-Hansen and his wife visited Ainola. They were received in the drawing-room, as was usual with guests, but I stayed in the library because I had at that time a particularly large assignment of work. Through the open door I heard Sibelius's lively talk with his guests, his amusing remarks and in general what an engaging host he was. About half-past four the visitors went and it was only then that I learned that Sibelius had had severe toothache. Two aspirins did nothing to help, and when I left in the late evening the tooth was still hurting. But Sibelius was pleased with himself: 'It was not all that easy to hide the pain from my visitors. I think I played the comedy very well and scarcely anyone noticed anything.'

Five weeks later, during the Sibelius Week, he bore pain with just as much fortitude. Elisabeth Schwarzkopf and her husband, as well as Yehudi Menuhin, Eugene Ormandy and all the Phila-delphia Orchestra were paying a visit to Ainola at that time. During the whole of the week the ninety-year-old master was plagued with toothache but none of the guests suspected it. The orchestra were assembled under the birch-trees in front of the villa. Sibelius went onto the veranda and said a few friendly words to the players: 'You are all outstanding artists,' he called to them.

A lot of ink has flowed in describing the magic of the composer's personality. His pupils and relations were able to say a great deal about it, and even quite casual visitors used to speak of the vital radiance that they felt in his presence.

His gracious behaviour to all people, even to those of least importance, undoubtedly went a long way to his winning all hearts. He had acquired this in childhood. Maria Sibelius, widowed at the age of twenty-seven, even though she was on her own had a good idea of bringing up her children properly. She took great pains in teaching them the most important and perhaps hardest thing of all, tact and delicacy in dealing with people. Even when he was a very old man Sibelius remembered his mother's teaching. He once received a floral greeting from South Africa, and I composed a letter of thanks in which I mentioned among other things that the spring flowers would soon be coming into bloom in Ainola. But Sibelius struck out the sentence. He said: 'We had better not say that. When I was a small boy a lady who knew my mother brought her some apples. We ourselves had more than enough, but my mother took me on one side and whispered in my ear that I was not to say a word about our own apples. And I have never forgotten that.'

He believed that his upbringing had been largely responsible for forming his character. 'I grew up without a father and was surrounded only by women. Perhaps this was the precise reason why I never learned how to have my own way, but from the start always to consider the feeling of others. If my fathers had brought me up I would perhaps have become quite otherwise.'

Sometimes he made a joke of his own behaviour and said that he was wretchedly old-fashioned: 'That was my so-called kindness of heart again. Others call it stupidity. In my youth the Topelian [1] view of life prevailed. One should be helpful and sincere and not think ill of one's fellow-men. Sacrificing love to duty if called upon to do so was taken for granted, but today one finds that all this kind of thing is considered laughable. It is just as well that I don't use the railway any more. I have heard that men keep their seats while old women are left standing. I would find it hard not to

[1] Zachris Topelius (1818–98), an influential Finnish writer.

give such "gentlemen" a clout on the ears. It would lead to a case
of "grievous bodily harm", and I would have to pay up. There's
no doubt but that I travel more cheaply by motor-car.'

The amiable disposition of the master, however, was inborn as
well as acquired by training. He did not find it burdensome to
provide pleasure for his fellow-men, and nothing was too good for
his guests. I had to laugh when Mrs Sibelius told me that her
husband had even reproached her for not having been sufficiently
attentive to guests. (She was, indeed, the best hostess I had ever
known.) Nor, after guests had gone, was Sibelius always entirely
pleased with himself. When he was young he once accompanied
General Järnefelt only as far as the door of the house and not to the
garden gate. He never forgot that. Every time he thought back on
the episode, even when he was very old, he was annoyed with
himself for having, as he thought, been lacking in courtesy
towards his father-in-law.

It was also very characteristic of Sibelius that he always most
warmly noticed the efforts of others. He understood that this gave
pleasure. In the course of the year the telephone line from Ainola
carried a great many words of encouragement. When a young
Finnish composer had had a concert Sibelius never forgot to
congratulate him, for he knew exactly how much his call pleased
the young man. He always had a kind word for artists who performed his works, even if it was a broadcast performance with
which he was not altogether satisfied. He consistently avoided
saying anything discouraging to anyone.

I used to win small prizes in photographic competitions and
sometimes these were announced in the press. If Sibelius noticed
one of these announcements he was always most warm in his
praises, just as if I had created a masterpiece. He would even
telephone me over such a trifle. If I published a new book—which
happened three times during his lifetime—Sibelius often referred
to it. He spoke with appreciation of its merits, and never a syllable
about its defects.

He who wishes to please his fellow-men without giving offence
to any must accustom himself to dealing with the truth with some
freedom. With Sibelius the use of white lies was second nature.

With a facility that always surprised me he discovered courteous phrases that acually had little real meaning. He joked about this:

> The truth is the most stupid thing to say to anyone. Others tell a lot more lies than I do, but what on earth would life be like if we all started throwing the 'truth' at each other's heads, as some appear to consider their privilege. We would have many really unhappy people. Quite apart from this all truth is subjective and therefore only to be seen as truth from one's own standpoint.

He spoke to me more than once about this matter. The problem of absolute truth had clearly concerned him. When Georg Kulenkampff, shortly before his untimely death, visited Sibelius for the last time, both masters talked not only about the fugues of Bach but also about honesty in society in all its aspects. They were touchingly in agreement. 'Whoever wishes to have anything to do with people must lie,' said Kulenkampff also. He was delighted when Sibelius told him how the schoolboys in Hämeenlinna had once resolved to tell each other nothing but the naked truth, and how the result was a wild free-for-all, the like of which the youngsters had never before experienced.

Sibelius also gave free play in his letters to his sense of fantasy. He would dictate an answer to a letter in which he would speak of the happy days of youth spent together; at the same time he would make a remark on the side for my benefit that he hadn't the slightest idea as to who the chap was. 'My letters,' he said, 'give a wrong impression of me. They are always attuned to what I think will best suit the person who gets them.' I often observed this. He knew how to formulate a refusal with delicacy, and there were not a few indifferent musicians who had encouragement from him in genial terms.

Sibelius realized that his civility sometimes collected worry and vexation for him. He used to say, 'I envy those who can unceremoniously rebuff those who want something from them. They have a much easier time than I.'

He could have put such a disposition to good use. The secretaries of famous men can tell of how much thoughtlessness,

arrogance, and plain naïveté we men are capable of. Almost everybody felt the urge to bother Finland's most celebrated citizen with
his own insignificant affairs. Sibelius had masses of inquiries and
requests that should have been addressed elsewhere, and a great
deal of the old master's time and energy was dissipated in such
irrelevancies. It would have been altogether simple if he had left
these things to his secretary, but unfortunately in each request he
saw a person whom he would not willingly rebuff.

It often happened that some unknown musician wanted to
rearrange a piece by Sibelius for his own instrument. Sibelius
almost always gave his consent. The arrangement then was often
so terrible that he could not approve it. Instead of simply forbidding its publication he gave himself the task of improving the
work. In the end not much remained of the original arrangement,
and Sibelius was no more satisfied. Finally he would give his
consent, suppressing his annoyance and saying: 'I wouldn't like to
discourage the poor man.'

From time to time the wishes of musicians can be very comic.
There was a Canadian clarinettist who wanted to know why he
couldn't go on playing to the end in the Second Symphony, but
had to stop before the last chord. 'If you really want to,' said
Sibelius, 'you can play quietly. You won't do any damage by this.'

Musicians, even the least gifted, were after all musicians. Letters
from fans, asking for no more than a few gramophone records,
were almost numberless, and they came with the most out-of-the-
way requests. Some correspondents thought that they should
discuss their affairs of the heart with their favourite composer. An
American couple wanted to be married in Ainola, and nowhere
else, while Mrs Sibelius once had to listen on the telephone to the
distress of a weeping girl whose fiancé had cleared off. Before
doing so he had said that he knew the great composer very well. A
young German woman once hinted that Sibelius should put her in
touch with a well-known sportsman, with whom she had fallen in
love in Finland.

There is no doubt that Sibelius would have been no bad
postillon d'amour. As a young man he had once even proposed on
behalf of a friend—with the best results, for it was a very happy

marriage. Another couple, wanting a divorce, came first to hear the views of the great man. 'In the event of Mr Sibelius wanting us to stay together we'll give it another try,' they said. Naturally this was what Sibelius suggested, comforting them with this thought: 'In what marriage are there no difficulties?' The divorce never took place.

These small occurrences, in themselves not so very significant, testify to the confidence which Sibelius aroused in all those who came near him. He was always prepared to believe only the best of his fellow-men and it was on this that the magic of his personality was based. He himself confessed: 'I idealize people. I allow them to have the finest qualities, which then turn out to be pure fancy.' But disappointments never altered him:

> The older I grow the more it seems to me that it is only the purely human factor that signifies anything. Differences of situation disappear. All classes, so far as I am concerned, are drawn to me. The longer I live the Finnish farmer especially comes more and more into my affection.

Even in early days the simple people had always been sympathetic to him. For many years he had a servant, named Heikki, at Ainola, with whom he liked to talk—particularly in the Sauna bath. Sibelius would sit in the tub and Heikki see to it that the water was kept warm enough. Master and servant could then quietly discuss all the problems of human existence while the moon shone through the small window in the bathroom. When we once discussed Heikki, who at that time had gone home to Karelia, Sibelius said: 'I would far rather talk to such simple people than with an Edvard Westermarck.' [1]

He was always interested in extraordinary characters and turns of fortune. 'My wife,' he said, 'thinks that all men of originality are dotty. I find them much more amusing than the general run of everyday people, of whom thirteen make a dozen. Besides, where is the boundary line?'

In this connection in many ways he asked too much of his wife. Once a tramp, with cuts all over him, turned up asking for

[1] Edvard Westermarck (1863–1939) was a well-known Finnish sociologist and philosopher.

charity. Sibelius called him into his room, talked with him about this and that, clothed him from head to foot in garments of his own that were by no means worn out, and finally put a hat on his head. As the man, overjoyed, left, Sibelius called his wife to the window. 'Look,' he said with pleasure, 'there goes Sibelius!'

In the course of his long life he had had a number of queer friends. 'Again and again I'm told that I should not appear in public with so-and-so,' he said. 'So far as I'm concerned they're all people, indeed, people of much interest.'

As a man he was just as individual and unusual as he was as a composer. It was difficult at times to follow his general train of thought. But combined with this originality there was a clear conservative strain in him; for he had a respect for his ancestors, for customs and for tradition. I often noticed how his was a somewhat twofold, divided, personality. To outward appearance there were two quite different people. On the one hand there was the patriarch with the proud gait, who commanded difficult situations with sovereign calm. But a quite different kind of Sibelius dwelt in the same man; the sensitive artist, with tender nerves, who could easily become impatient and querulous over insignificant details. His moods could change surprisingly quickly, for no apparent reason.

One day, speaking of himself, Sibelius said to me: 'My character has something demonic about it, that I feel very strongly from time to time; but all the same there is a childish strain to compensate for it.' One hardly ever saw the demonic side of his character, which for the most part showed itself in his music, but the boyishness was very evident in the old days. Mrs Sibelius and the other members of the family gave many affecting examples. Particularly in his earlier years, his life was frequently marked by a childlike carelessness, such as is only to be discovered in artists. Among the countless press cuttings that were sent to Ainola from all over the world there was one that presented the Finnish master as a correct, solid citizen. Sibelius read the article and then said: 'You've no idea what a Bohemian I used to be when I was young.' He recalled how he had once arrived home from Germany in dress clothes, and went over the adventure once more, chuckling all the time:

It was like this. After I had had my allowance from Finland I entertained my friends in Berlin right royally. There wasn't a penny left over. So I sold, or pawned (I don't rightly know which), all the rest of my clothes and put on a dress-suit for my journey home. A steamer used to go in those days from Stettin to Visby, and it was an expensive journey. It was certainly rather embarrassing to appear next morning in Stockholm in a crumpled dress-suit and dirty shirt. But I had friends there who helped me out of my difficulty.

This carelessness of the 'artistic temperament' now and then showed itself in somewhat doubtful ways. It could happen that the composer turned up at some concert he was to conduct the worse for drink, to imagine himself at rehearsal. In the middle of the work he would knock off with a show of vigour, command repetition of the whole lot, turn round and try to quieten the audience—suffocating with laugher—with hissing noises and comic gesticulations. He arrived too late at a concert of his own works in Copenhagen, where King Christian X was present. Sibelius regretted this all his life, because it was tactless behaviour towards the Danes and their King. But King Christian did not take offence and had a friendly talk with the composer.

One may also describe the master's clumsiness in all practical matters as a by-product of the careless side of his temperament. Doing things with his hands whether as a hobby or for some specific purpose was not up his street. Mrs Sibelius had to look after everything and to help him in the smallest details of the daily round. Nor was tidiness a strong suit with him. Without the help of the ever-alert ladies of Ainola he probably would never have been able to find anything. Letters and other papers disappeared for long periods—if not for ever. From time to time he laughed at his helplessness.

As we once tried in vain to find an important letter, he said:

Once more we have the most unbelievable state of disorder here. When I die my heirs are going to have one hell of a job going through everything. I have never learned how to keep my things tidy. As sure as I take extra good care of something, it vanishes—until, to my astonishment, it turns up in some quite other, strange place. Just lately I was turning the leaves of an old bible and a 100-Mark note fell out. It must have been hidden away for ages. Anyway it had long been made valueless.

In self-defence let me say here that, even though I was his secretary, I was never allowed to tidy the table on which the master worked. There were some things that he insisted on dealing with personally, whether he did them well or badly. He had a container of his own, the so-called 'green box', that no one was allowed to touch. All the letters and papers that interested him particularly went into it. They often stayed there for months. Letters that had been dealt with long ago were also always turning up again in the 'green box'.

As well as all this good nature Sibelius could surprisingly show quite contrary characteristics. In respect of his compositions he knew himself to be his own most severe critic and he was never content unless every note was precisely as he had intended. Even in quite everyday things he could in fact appear to be pedantic. If the vase of flowers was not directly under the light, but was a little to the side, it got on his nerves. It had to be in the middle. His slippers had to be put in the right way under his bed—with the heels turned outward, otherwise Sibelius couldn't sleep. Some things he looked after with special care, particularly if they had come from one of his relatives of whom he had been fond.

So far as his clothes were concerned Sibelius was no Bohemian, but a well-set-up gentleman who took care that everything was in apple-pie order. I never once saw him badly shaved even though in later years he could scarcely shave himself because of his shaking hands, and it was only towards the very end that he occasionally appeared in slippers. His individuality and sense of fantasy never showed themselves in his mode of dress.

Much more interesting than these externals, however, was the old master's attitude to the real facts of life. He saw everything with astonishing clarity and always went at once to the heart of the matter. He had no large illusions about the potentials of thought. 'The range of our understanding,' he said, 'is very limited. Immanuel Kant pressed towards the furthest limits. But how much did he actually know? Practically nothing.' Sibelius himself had an intuitive kind of intellect, by means of which he came to quick and certain conclusions. It was surprising, however, that his lively imagination did not lead him into error, but that he always looked for the plain facts. He told me that himself on many occasions.

This need to see everything in life in the clearest light determined his relationship to the present time in an interesting way. He was eighty when he once said to me:

> It doesn't make sense to embellish and to explain facts simply because they appear to be strange to us old people. One should face the trends of our time with open eyes. I am always taking the trouble to find out what's happening, and that makes it easy for me to understand the present. It is very hard for my wife. She grumbles about the revolutionary changes of our time and can't rid herself of the past. As for me, the older I grow the more I want to see what is ahead. Today's endeavours aren't at all alien to me. I can get on with them very well.

Marshall McLuhan, the philosopher of the electronic age, should have said that we men always live in the past. It is only artists who live in the present. In old age many of us are even hostile to modern ideas. That that was never the case with Sibelius is the more remarkable since inevitably many things had to remain unfamiliar to him. There was at that time no television in Finland, and in the whole of his life he never saw a sound film. He had never travelled on a bus, let alone an aeroplane. More than once he asked me questions which showed an unawareness of very many things that were then commonplace. Under these circumstances it was very surprising how much interest he took in what was going on. This extended to his relationship with modern music, as I shall explain at a later point.

He was like this to the end. There was but one occasion on which I heard him lament the passing of 'the good old days'—as old people for the most part do—and even then he only spoke in jest. I was in Ainola with a young Brazilian journalist (whose field was culture) who had come to interview Sibelius. In the course of the conversation the journalist told how a single tribe of man-eaters still lived in a primeval forest in Brazil. The government allowed them to live in peace, although all missionaries were eaten up by the cannibals. Once a year the President flew over the area symbolically to show that the tribe belonged to the State of Brazil. It sometimes happened that afterwards when the plane had landed, arrows were found on it.

Sibelius had been listening attentively, and suddenly his face took on a roguish expression. He laughed and said: 'I have had need of man-eaters in recent times. The romance of the last century more and more disappears. Much was lost when the Turkish harems were closed, and the cannibals certainly belong to the good old days.'

For lunch we had partridge—the master's favourite dish. He was in the best of moods, cut himself a portion of partridge, took a draught of red wine, and all of a sudden said: 'How splendid that there are still cannibals.'

FIVE

ᐅᐅ

The sixth sense

I suppose that most, if not all, artists have particularly sensitive instincts. In the case of Sibelius these were more strongly developed than with ordinary men, as I found many times.

In matters of cooking he was a connoisseur and as such was complimented even by the experts in the best restaurants. He was acquainted with all delicacies up to grasshoppers and swallows' nests. He quoted many examples of his sensitivity of feeling. Generally speaking he could not use cotton sheets, because they irritated his skin too much. His sense of smell was also particularly strongly developed. As Walter von Konow, the superintendent of the Turku Museum, former schoolmate and lifelong friend of the composer, has said, Sibelius was musically excited—even when he was a schoolboy—by his sense of smell. Scents and aromas had a very clear influence on his spirits. If he was nervous a few drops of eau-de-Cologne could work wonders. Sometimes, if he was unable to sleep, he wiped it all over his body.

From time to time I noticed that his other senses, principally that of sight, affected his feelings of smell and taste. One day I brought a picture book of the Finnish Photographic Society to Ainola. Sibelius turned over the pages for a while and then studied a very fine winter landscape with particular care. 'How strange,' he suddenly said. 'When I bury myself deep in this picture I can quite distinctly smell the snow.' Anything he particularly disliked was as 'the taste of metal' in his mouth.

As was proper to the great musician, his sense of hearing was most strongly developed. He had absolute pitch, which was not the case with all great composers—Schumann and Wagner, for instance. I was able to establish this in my first weeks with Sibelius when I hummed a few bars from a Schubert symphony.

'That's a semitone too high,' he said. As courteous as ever, he added: 'Anyone who has perfect pitch can make as much error as that.'

I assured him that I hadn't got perfect pitch, but that after taking due care, and when it was necessary, I could just about recognize a clear case of C major. It was a pure fluke that I had got so near.

For Sibelius it was not only in music that notes and tonalities were to be heard. They were about everywhere. The curlew, whose lament sounded out on warm summer evenings from the broad meadows around Ainola, sang between *a* and *f*. Speaking as an old violinist, Sibelius said that the bullfinch 'double-stopped'. Mostly he sang *c* sharp–*d*, but a larger bullfinch twittered away between *d* and *d* sharp. Even in commonplace noises Sibelius heard musical sounds. When the veranda was being repaired one day and a loud hammering came from there into the library Sibelius said: 'The man is all the time hitting a *g* that is about a quarter-tone out of tune.'

Colours had a great deal of significance for him. He experienced them as musical sounds, not merely approximating to, but actually possessing, exact pitch. They were not limited only to tones and semitones. I once asked him which note was represented by his favourite colour—a clear green. He was able to answer me at once: 'It's somewhere between *d* and *e* flat.' Then he sang the note to me and went to the piano to check it. He had got it exactly. For *d* was a shade lower than the note he had sung, and *e* flat noticeably higher. Sibelius always said that this favourite colour of his, that had more of yellow than blue in it, was not to be found anywhere in his environment. He had only seen it, and then but seldom, in the sky. He said: 'I believe that it belongs to an earlier age and not to our time at all.'

I would have liked to note down the colours of all the keys as they were seen by Sibelius, but I never did; the old master was always too impatient for anything systematic. However, I did get to know that related keys—like C major and A minor, and (in a different way) C major and minor—had entirely different colours. It was interesting that one key could also have two colours. Sibelius once said to me that B flat major suggested to him 'something blue-yellow'; and another time, 'B major is a glaring red.' I also recall him saying:

> In my parents' house in Hämeenlinna there was a bright carpet on the floor. I was always trying to find the corresponding notes on the piano. I can very well remember how we got our first piano. Before then we had had a 'table piano'. The new instrument was brown and made a G major impression. Immediately, then, I played on it in G major.

In the summer of 1948 Thomas Beecham made a new recording of *Tapiola*, and, as usual, sent a copy to Ainola. When I heard it, Sibelius had played the record twice and was not altogether pleased. 'The strings are too weak,' he said. 'In addition to that, here and there he has given too much prominence to the parts at the expense of the *ensemble*. There are also some pauses which I don't like.' After we had listened to the record together he asked my opinion. I said that with the exception of a few bars I liked it very much. That seemed to please him. He added, 'This time I found it a good deal better.' Then he went to the window and looked awhile at the evening sky. 'All colours seem different to me now, after hearing *Tapiola*,' he said softly.

Colours always affected his moods. Grey chocolate thoroughly depressed him. So did venison soup mixed with black-currant juice. A particular blue bank-note always put him out of sorts. Bright colours on the other hand cheered him up. A new red silk cloth gave him especial pleasure. He called me into his bedroom and showed it to me, saying: 'Every morning when I wake up I enjoy myself looking at this beautiful colour.'

One afternoon shortly before his birthday we were standing at the window and looking towards the distant Tuusula Lake, where the pale light of the winter evening faintly illuminated the open landscape. Sibelius spoke about the colours of nature:

> An artist, even the greatest, can't reproduce them. They have a life of their own, that one can't transfer to canvas. We are just as limited in our looking at colours. We can say: 'I call this

bright green', but we don't know whether other people see colours exactly or precisely as we do. It's the same with notes. No one is able to say how he hears a note. Not only this, but there are many notes which we can't use in music at all.

Sibelius contemplated the darkened landscape for a while in silence. Then he went on:

> As I have mentioned before, I believe that there are musical notes and harmonies on all planets. Naturally men live on them too, although probably they have a quite other form than ours and lead a quite different existence. It is laughable to imagine that our small planet is the only one to have life.

I noticed more than once that Sibelius was not dependent only on five senses. It was often astonishing how he was aware of things that must have been quite unknown to him. At least twice he had a premonition that I was ill, and once he telephoned me on that account, although by normal human means of understanding he could have had no occasion to do so. In fact I was in bed with a high temperature, but no one except my wife knew.

Mrs Sibelius firmly believed that her husband knew when any of his works were to be broadcast anywhere in the world. She said: 'He is sitting quietly, reading a book or a newspaper. Suddenly he becomes restless, goes to the radio, turns the knobs, and then one of his symphonies or tone-poems comes out of the air.'

One day when I had just arrived and we had settled ourselves round the coffee-table, Sibelius quite irrelevantly asked: 'Have you brought your camera with you?'

That was a most surprising question. I never had a camera with me when I went to work at Ainola. If I wanted to take pictures, we came to an agreement beforehand. Sibelius was then able to prepare himself in advance.

But what was most remarkable was that on this particular day there actually was a quite new camera in the pocket of my overcoat in the ante-room. The day before I had made a chance purchase and I now wanted to christen my new camera, so to speak, by taking some pictures at Ainola. But Sibelius could have had no knowledge of that.

I was to have a second surprise at once. I fetched the camera from the ante-room and showed it to him. He examined it—surely out of politeness, for he knew nothing about photography and cameras. This kind of thing didn't interest him at all. But suddenly he asked: 'A camera like this must cost a small fortune—40,000 more or less?'

I had paid exactly 40,000 marks. If he had said 50,000 that would have been a nice round sum. But why had he calculated 40,000? Sibelius was himself amazed when I told him that he had hit the nail precisely on the head.

'That was indeed comic! How could I have known? I haven't the slightest idea what cameras like this cost.'

In the course of his long life he had had many much more remarkable experiences. Many men when they visit a strange place for the first time suddenly have the peculiar feeling that they have already been there at some time or another. But Sibelius—to whom this sort of thing frequently happened—knew exactly round which street corner, for example, there was a tobacconist's shop.

One day he told me of how, as a very young man and although he was then often ill, he had known he was to live a long time. He assured me with some fervour that he knew, not merely felt, that this would be so:

> In a meeting I once said that everybody who was there would be dead before me. Naturally they protested that no one could know that precisely, and how had I come to say what I had said with such certainty. I knew it with complete certainty, and they're all long since dead.

Shortly after his eighty-fifth birthday Sibelius said to me quite spontaneously: 'In five years' time I shall be ninety!' That he might die before then didn't seem to occur to him. At the same time he told me that he had long felt that something of great importance would soon take place in the world. 'Perhaps it will be in some years' time, but it will come.'

Sibelius used to like to talk about supernatural matters, which interested him greatly, and he was not confined by any kind of prejudice. Everything was possible so far as he was concerned—a full half-century before science extended the limits of what is possible almost to infinity. He said:

How childish it is to imagine that with our tiny brain we can comprehend everything in the universe. That was already clear to me when I was young. I remember a group of doctors who, at the end of the last century, used regularly to dine at the same table in a well-known restaurant. They knew everything—for the most part problems for them didn't exist. 'That is impossible'; 'That isn't so': these were their favourite arguments. Then the Curies discovered radium, and the gentlemen were in very low spirits. 'I must start all over again,' one of them honestly admitted.

Sibelius had a very active dream life, which often used to surprise his doctor. Old people dream infrequently, but Sibelius was exceptional in that respect also. The next morning he was able to describe exactly what he had seen. This characteristic, like so many others, was inherited from his mother. Maria Sibelius even had dreams that came true. Every time before she was seriously ill she saw herself going into church, and shortly before her death she dreamed very clearly that she was taking Holy Communion.

Sibelius also heard a great deal of music in dreams, by which he was often much moved. But when he woke up the music had for the most part dissolved into something completely banal and useless. As violinist he once achieved a fantastic masterpiece in a dream, but by the time he was awake it had become a complete impossibility.

Sibelius told me that his dreams were very clear to him, and the colours particularly always had intensity and radiance. He lived a new life in his dreams, encountered many people and saw splendid landscapes and strange cities. Sometimes he experienced high drama in his dreams, especially in extreme old age. He could go through great stretches of time in the same night. Once he spent some months in Japan although the period of dreaming was limited to hours. In the morning he even remembered that his correspondence was forwarded to him to a *poste restante* and that each day he fetched his letters from the post office. He dreamed a great deal about Japan, although he had never been there. He was always in the same place—in a large square. He had no money left, and didn't know how he should pay the Japanese who had driven him in his cart. The square was always the same but the time varied. New buildings appeared that had not been there in earlier dreams. Every time he wondered from whom he could get money and if, maybe, the Finnish Consulate or Embassy was in the neighbourhood. He often had the notion that he could write something in order to pay the driver of the cart. He also once found himself moneyless in London, in addition to which he had forgotten the name of his hotel. In the end his son-in-law appeared and gave him a little money, but seemed not to be particularly interested in his problem.

Sometimes his dreams were so comic that next morning he had to have a good laugh. One night he became the owner of a merry-go-round and had some important clients. The Danish Ambassador rode on a little pony and the wife of the Finnish President, Paasikivi, sat on a white poodle. His good Havana cigars more often than not went out during his dreams—which caused Sibelius much concern.

He had bad nightmares only when he was a child, and one of them recurred time after time. When guests came to stay for the night—which was frequently the case when there was a storm or bad snow—the boy had to sleep in the attic. When he did he always had the same horrible dream. The door opened onto the dark earth and a dismal group of black monks brought a coffin into the room. They came quite near, and several touched the boy's face, who was beside himself with fear and woke up in a bath of perspiration.

When he was awake the boy was very much afraid of the dark too, and this fear also afflicted him in later life. If there was no light his lively imagination began to play. Sibelius several times told me that in the night he had seen blue hands, which had stretched out after him. 'I am not at all ashamed,' he said, 'that I don't like the dark. All men with quick imaginations are aware of that fear.'

Even in the clear light of day Sibelius could experience remarkable visions. Once when he was sitting by himself in his favourite chair in the library the opposite wall suddenly vanished and in its place a broad expanse of sandy shore appeared. He heard the splash of the waves and felt the warmth of the sun. There were two young girls walking along the shore and speaking English.

A vision of this sort is easy to explain if one believes that Sibelius had fallen asleep for a brief moment. But he assured me that there was no doubt about his being awake, and added that, what was more, he hadn't taken one drop of alcohol. According to his reckoning the vision lasted for about ten seconds.

A second vision of which Sibelius told me was much more remarkable, giving proof at least of an almost eerie power of imagination. Once in Paris he went with a group of tourists into the Palace of Versailles. He stayed for a moment alone in the room in which the ruler had died, while the rest of the group went on. Suddenly he saw the last hours of a French king. He remembered this: 'I could not clearly see the dead man himself, but I saw everybody else who was in the room—the prelates and courtiers—and I even sensed the odour of death. It was horribly unpleasant. I don't like such macabre things one bit.'

One evening in the February of 1950 as Sibelius and I sat together in the library he told me that he had had an extraordinary experience in the last few days.

'I suddenly fell under the influence of an unknown force that I can neither recognize nor control. It is very tiresome.'

'Is it,' I asked, 'some sort of vision?'

'No, no! It's nothing like what happened in Versailles. It's something that we do not know at all.'

'Does it happen in the night?'

'And in the day too. So far I have experienced this twice. I have not said anything to my wife about it. It is frightfully unpleasant.'

Like Haydn and Mozart, Sibelius was a Freemason and as such he achieved very high rank. It was seldom, if ever, that he spoke in any kind of detail about questions of faith or philosophy of life, but the religion of a divinely gifted artist is in essence identical with his art. He once said when we were talking about Anton Bruckner, 'All great men—each in his own way—are deeply religious.' The need for belief in God was something that seemed to him self-evident, and in his opinion it was only lacking in those whose thought was at a very primitive level. Of one Swedish writer he said:

Just like the mentality of a schoolboy, who feels that anything as sublime as religion is ridiculous. How a man can get along without religion I can't understand. Life is full of enigmas, and the older I grow the more I perceive how precious little we actually know. The mysteries are always increasing.

On the highest spot in the woods of Ainola, an exposed rock, Sibelius once wanted to build an altar. He had already talked the matter over with a well-known sculptor. 'It was to have been a gesture to the Power Above,' he said, as we stood on the rock one day and talked about the project, which never came to fulfilment. 'The fact that man believes and always has believed in God, proves in my opinion that a higher Being rules all that is—how and in what form we cannot naturally know.' Once when we spoke about the purpose of art Sibelius quite spontaneously said: 'The essence of man's being is his striving after God.'

Sibelius held fast to the belief that he was under the protection of an invisible power. During his long life so much had happened that he could not otherwise account for. More than once his life was in danger and was saved by chance.

In New York he nearly fell into the clutches of gangsters. He had asked his chauffeur to drive him to a restaurant, and the man, realizing at once that he had a helpless foreigner in the car, drove into a dark cul-de-sac where he stopped in front of a dubious little bar. It was deep in a cellar, with steep steps leading down. At the bottom stood a dissolute looking gangster figure who was weighing up his visitors with appraising looks. Sibelius was already halfway down when it suddenly became clear to him that he was going to be lured into a trap. With a leap he was back in the street, and he ran away from the place without looking round.

A similar incident occurred to him in Berlin. He came to a very out-of-the-way restaurant late one night and had already ordered his meal when a total stranger whispered a warning into his ear. It was dangerous for foreigners to eat there, he said. Clients at night ran the risk of being doped and robbed.

In the autumn of 1920 Sibelius by chance met a well-known Finnish airman, Major Väinö Mikkola, who was on the point of going to Italy with two young officers to bring back two Savoia machines for the Finnish State. Major Mikkola told the composer of his mission and proposed that he should go with him. The flight over the Alps at that time would have been a rare experience, and Major Mikkola assured Sibelius that it would be entirely without danger. He asserted many times: 'Nothing can go wrong.'

Sibelius wanted very much to go on this flight but fortunately was not able to do so, thereby avoiding certain death. Both machines crashed in the Alps and all the airmen were killed. Eyewitnesses testified that they had seen the machines explode in the air, and immediately the question of sabotage was raised. No proof, however, could be found and the accident remained a mystery. When he talked to me about the airmen Sibelius said: 'Chance and good luck are insufficient in themselves to explain how it is that my life was preserved. A greater Power has one in its protection.'

In that Sibelius was a man of the utmost kindness it may be said that he intuitively knew the substance of traditional teaching on brotherly love. In this fundamental sense he was truly Christian but formal expressions of religion had no meaning for him. He never went to church, for it went against his nature to make a public display of piety or devotion. As a rule it was difficult for him to expose his innermost thoughts to others.

When the Oxford Movement first got under way in Finland Sibelius remarked, 'I have always feared that I could fall victim to this kind of revivalism. What a frightful idea, that I should go before a great congregation to confess my sins! Really! I wouldn't confess a thing!' At the same time he acknowledged that he had some sympathy with the members of the Oxford Group since they did not sit autocratically and idly by but were always busy and achieving a good deal.

'I too have my own religion,' he said when once we spoke of the fact that his mother and only sister had both been deeply religious. The supernatural element in Christian dogmatics and even the basic teaching of Christianity did not seem to signify a great deal to him. 'Christ,' he once cried out, 'must have been a wonderful man.' Then he suddenly fell silent and laughed to himself. 'I would never have dared to say that in my parents' house. My mother knew nothing worse than that one should deny the divinity of the Saviour.'

A religious musical friend once wrote a long letter to Sibelius in which he spoke about the Second Coming of the Redeemer. After I had given him some idea of the contents of this letter Sibelius said: 'It is to be hoped that He doesn't come. I am convinced that they would crucify Him for a second time.'

What then was his own religion? I believe that it was strongly pantheistic and very much bound up with his life's work. 'There is music in the whole universe,' he said, and twice he told me how the Almighty had revealed Himself to him.

At the beginning of December 1946 the weather was particularly gloomy and rough, on account of which Sibelius went out very little. When I came to Ainola a few days before his birthday the sun again peeped through the mass of clouds, for the first time for ages. 'How marvellous,' said Sibelius, 'even this weak sunshine is. What peace and deep devotion Nature can arouse in man!' Then he spoke about the astonishing sense of law in the universe, and an almost inconceivable harmony that makes every human effort seem tiny and senseless. 'That,' he concluded, 'is precisely what I call God.'

Some years later we were once speaking about religious sects that just then for this or that reason were in the news. Sibelius said, 'Naturally each one of us has his own concept of God. I have always found that the Almighty reveals Himself to me most clearly through my musical understanding, in that wonderful artistic logic that I seldom notice as I compose but can recognize afterwards—when the composition is finished.'

This sense of pantheistic eternity resounds powerfully in the Finnish master's best works, where it springs from within the recesses of his soul. He has very movingly set these words of Viktor Rydberg in one of his most beautiful songs (Op. 38, no. 2):

Dost know the stillness,
That submerges everything as in an eternity of longing—
The shores, the heavens, the sea
In one thought of God.

In nature and in his own creations—which were ever closely

bound together—Sibelius therefore had the clearest impression of the presence of the Almighty. Very few men have such an intimate relationship with nature as he had, and all his life it was a source of inspiration and joy. Several times he told me how intensely he had been affected by quite small natural occurrences even as a child:

> I am no longer the same as I was then. I am even unable now to approach the flowers as I did when I was a child. I almost have the feeling that they consider me blameworthy. Then I lived in nature. Even today I remember some dense grass that grew high above my head, and how I felt that I was within the grass and that I had entirely grown up within it.

He often used to have a match-box filled with moss with him, for through the scent of the moss he found it possible to transport himself into the atmosphere of the woods. Sometimes he would lie on his stomach under a bush so that he could inhale deeply the scent of the bare earth. This gave him a great sense of well-being. Later in life he kept his handkerchiefs in a box made out of juniper wood.

The intensity of his love of nature appeared to be in no way diminished in old age. 'The change of the seasons is today the most important thing in my life,' he said to me when he was approaching the age of ninety. In the summer he often woke up at four o'clock to see the changing colours of the sky as the sun disappeared and reappeared. He would go from room to room and, standing by the window that faced south, would enjoy this great dramatic performance on the part of nature. For he could also imagine that he saw his own particular shade of green in the sky. He would say: 'So one glance banishes all cares.'

During the active part of his life he had had plenty of opportunity to admire the natural beauties of different countries. A landscape near Brünn, which he saw from a railway carriage window on his way to Italy, made the deepest impression on him. He also talked a great deal about the English countryside. He had never forgotten how mighty oak trees and bluebells grew there against a background of green-tinted sky and white clouds. But nothing could beat the bright trunks of the birch trees and the silent lakes of Finland. 'The older I grow,' he said to Count von

Rosen, who had travelled the five continents, 'the more I like my own country.'—'That's the case with me too,' answered von Rosen. Once we talked about how there were people without either imagination or sense of beauty. No sooner do they see a stately tree than they consider whether or not it is good for building. 'People like this,' said Sibelius, 'are already in control. But they are the unluckiest of people, for they have lost what is most important.'

Everywhere he saw beauty that was hidden from others. Quite small things in nature could stimulate colourful imagery in him. One evening he came home from the woods and, all excited, told his wife how he had seen some snowdrops that reminded him of a choir of children at prayer. That was not merely a fugitive idea, but something which, though small, was a real experience. He told me about it when I came to see him next day.

He was also capable of experiencing very vivid impressions through his imagination. One evening as we were walking in the garden he touched with his stick a pansy that had a broad white rim and four black dots in the middle. 'That,' he said, 'is Anton Sitt.' I looked at the flower and it was indeed the spitting image of the old leader of the city orchestra—with his white artist's mane and his dark eyebrows.

There were so many experiences of nature that indelibly imprinted themselves on his memory. More than once he pictured scenes to me with great enthusiasm—scenes that at some time or other years before had impressed him. He seemed to have the eye of a painter, composing pictures with a sure hand, and often with a strong dramatic sense.

For instance, there was the striking memory of a pheasant that one evening had taken flight against the background of a blue-black sky, its colourful feathers dazzling in the light of the last rays of the sun. In the early days in Järvenpää he had once been in the garden at two o'clock in the morning and had heard the cuckoo, the curlew and the wood-pigeon all at the same time. He never forgot. Even as an old man he used to recall how the cuckoo had sung 'out of tune', neither major nor minor, but something in between.

Sibelius was very interested in bird-song, about which we frequently talked. He had, for example, noticed that the great titmouse and the starling could easily imitate different sounds. 'When the starlings come from the south in the spring I can tell at once which have stayed in industrial districts and listened to the factory sirens,' he would say.

Perhaps the song of the birds had some significance so far as his compositions were concerned. A note made on Villa-Lobos's music is relevant to this: 'One can hear that he was brought up in a quite different bird world from me. In Brazil there are parrots, which have a penetrating sound. The ear gets accustomed to such a cutting tone very soon.'

He had himself seen in the Zoo in Berlin a parrot from the River Amazon that had a glaring yellow beak and screamed the interval of a seventh in a permanent *forte*. Sibelius, of course, would not claim that Villa-Lobos had made use of bird-song as such in his compositions. So far as he was concerned all twittering and cawing noises in music were an abomination, unless treated as in Beethoven's Pastoral Symphony.

The call of the crane, however, he described as 'the *Leitmotiv* of my life'. The flight of the migrant birds each spring and autumn was an important event for him. Everybody in Järvenpää knew that, and whenever swans or cranes came into sight he was immediately told—often by telephone. In earlier times he had taken long walks to see his favourite swans. It was certain that when they had settled down on the Lake of Tuusula he went down to welcome them. Often he ordered a taxi for this purpose.

Perhaps this great love of his for birds was connected with his only memory of the father whom he had lost so early in life. He remembered how he had sat in his father's lap and looked at a picture of a large swan.

One lovely spring day I had just arrived at Ainola when a great flock of white swans approached. We knew the direction from which they would come, for the neighbours had once again taken care of that. Actually we had something very important to discuss, but Sibelius promptly forgot that and went out on the veranda. There he stood in silence, his gaze directed to the heavens, as if he had expected a great miracle. But this time he waited in vain. Finally he said:

> They have flown over the lake. I can't see them, but I breathe the same air as they do, and that is something. Nobody has any idea what the flight of the migrant birds in the spring and autumn means to me. Once they were very late. On Christmas Eve a flock of about fifty swans flew very low over our house. I could hardly have thought of a better Christmas present for myself.

SIX

▷▷▷

The pressure of the commonplace

Nature had blessed Sibelius with rich gifts of intellect, but one talent—regarded by people today as most important—was for ever denied to him: he had absolutely no inclination towards economic affairs or any kind of practical thought.

His father had been helpless in these respects too. Dr Christian Sibelius frittered away his money in a free and easy manner and with no thought for security, and he was permanently head over heels in debt. At the time of his death what he owed amounted to 4,500 marks—a tidy sum for those days. His widow was made a technical bankrupt and she could only just save what was most needful for herself and her children.

From his father Sibelius inherited much that was creditable, but he was also endowed with his father's carelessness about money, and his upbringing did nothing to remove this defect of character. Although he had lost his father when he was only two, he spent his youth without any need to think about his living. He was twenty-seven before he earned any money of his own, at which, as an old man, he used to express surprise.

'It never occurred to me when I was a young man that I could earn anything by myself. In those days even the sons of the best families—Bertel Gripenberg, for example [1]—used to work as private tutors. But I found it perfectly in order that my poor mother should support me. It was unfeeling—but that never crossed my mind.'

Sibelius had a State grant of 2,000 marks for the period of study

---

[1] Bertel Gripenberg (1878–1947), nobleman and Finnish poet, some of whose poems were set to music by Sibelius.

that he commenced in Berlin in September 1889. But by November the money was gone and cries of help began to be directed towards Finland. Shocked, his family had to do everything for him—including selling his brother's old trousers—so that they could give him the money necessary to keep him through the winter. He was, and he remained as most artists are, a child of the moment—spendthrift, generous and unpractical. Saving and planning for the future were strange notions to him. If he had any money he got rid of it, even forgetting his family.

When he had been abroad on a concert tour he seldom brought anything home. It is true that he didn't earn much since he had to be responsible for his own expenses, but a considerable sum would often have remained over if he had not dissipated the lot. In Copenhagen he once gave five concerts that were all sold out. As he himself told me, he earned something like 6,000 marks which in those days was a great deal of money. Mrs Sibelius in Ainola heard that he had been very successful and lived in happy anticipation of the day when she would finally pay their debts and the eternal need of money would disappear, at least for a time. But it turned out to be a vain hope. Sibelius had amused himself day and night, had entertained those he knew and those he didn't know in lordly manner, and had acquired 'masses of new friends'. The 6,000 marks disappeared in a flash. Soon afterwards a Danish restaurateur ran into difficulties. 'Now that Jean Sibelius has departed,' wrote a Copenhagen newspaper, 'the place has gone bankrupt.'

Once he came from Italy to Innsbruck without a penny in his purse and had to break his journey. But instead of looking about for a cheap *pension* he went to a luxury hotel and immediately ordered a feast—the most expensive delicacies and wines, the best that the house could offer. The hotel manager was delighted and, thinking him to be a millionaire, treated him like a king. Luckily the money that he had ordered from Finland by telegram arrived after a few days. The 'millionaire' could pay his astronomically high bill and dispense princely tips, and escape home with what was left.

All economic concepts were hidden away from the old master in an impenetrable darkness. He used to joke about it. 'What ought one actually to understand by "invest"?' he asked me one day. 'I daren't ask my son-in-law, the bank director, or he'll think me an idiot.'

When he was an old man Sibelius had to have expensive hard liquor for his favourite guests, and the bills were correspondingly high. One day he told me that he never exactly knew what he actually had to pay. First came a delivery note and a good deal later the bill. In the meantime he had more bits of paper. He was never clear whether a bill was in order or not. 'Apparently they use duplicate Italian book-keeping methods there,' he said with a laugh. He had no kind of idea of book-keeping—of Italian or of any other sort; he only thought that it was something very artful. Once it really did happen that he was charged twice for a consignment. The correction came promptly with many expressions of regret and apologies. But from that day on the old master could not be quite convinced that he had not permanently become a victim of the duplicate Italian book-keeping system.

Once he did in fact discuss a possible commercial undertaking. His idea was so amusing that I immediately made a note of it. We were talking about volcanic areas, and the master's imagination produced this: 'If I had a lot of money I would establish luxury hotels here in Finland, in which would be available all that some millionaire or other can want. Then I would recruit guests for my hotels in those countries where the moneyed aristocrats live in permanent fear of earthquakes.'

With the exception of the last few decades, Sibelius was all his life in economic difficulties. What else could his helplessness and his generosity produce except continued trouble? One of his daughters said: 'Actually Daddy was always looking for money.' According to the living standards of the educated class his income was not particularly large, but nevertheless it was large enough to support an ordered, if modest, life. At first he was a music teacher, but very soon he received from the State an artist's grant—which later was considerably increased—for life. In the course of the years he received a number of honorariums and prizes. His friends also subsidized him in several ways. Baron Axel Carpelan, one of his greatest admirers and himself quite poor, not only gave him the necessary travelling expenses (5,000 marks) for a long holiday in the south, but later on let him have a quarterly allowance.

The income from concerts of his compositions was not to be despised, and there was further a regular, if not very great, source of revenue in the contracts with his publishers. Sibelius was unable to look after his interests to the best advantage, since the perpetual need for money had compelled him to sell all his compositions for lump sums. The *Valse Triste* and *Finlandia* alone would probably have made him a fortune if he had drawn up contracts on a royalty basis.

He once did have the chance to be royally remunerated for a composition, but he refused it. When Carl Stoeckel asked Sibelius after the Music Festival in Norfolk how much he was in debt to the composer for the first performance of *Oceanides* Sibelius asked for 1,000 dollars. That was much too little, and he immediately understood this when he noticed the disappointment of his patron. So far as Carl Stoeckel, the multi-millionaire, was concerned, the actual sum was neither here nor there. On the other hand he did not care to think that the principal work commissioned solely for his Music Festival was cheap. 'I should have said $5,000,' said Sibelius. 'But he could not offer more than I had asked, and so I had to make do with my $1,000. Anyway, that was then a lot of money to me.'

The unfavourable contracts of his youth from time to time appeared to depress him: no longer on his own account, but because they could have meant a good deal for his heirs. He was particularly concerned that his contracts also included all rights in respect of American performances and that these consequently came to the publishers.

One day when he was again talking about his 'bottomless stupidity' Mrs Sibelius came into the room and interrupted him: 'Why do you go on thinking about those unfortunate contracts? Nothing can be altered now. At the time you had no choice, you had to sell, for we had to live. The whole matter is no more of any consequence whatever. Every year everything is better, and we can thank God that all has turned out so well.' Sibelius laughed, and, for a moment forgetting all his contracts, said, 'You speak exactly like my mother.'

At that time a great deal was being written in the world's press about the composer's American performance rights. Olin Downes, the American music critic, published a detailed article on the subject in the *New York Times* which caused something of a sensation. A number of Americans, friends as well as people unknown to him, offered to do something about it and I remember that Sibelius did in fact get part of the American royalties which had accumulated in America during the war.

Touching letters came from the United States. One fan wrote something like this:

> I hear that you don't get a farthing for the performances of your works in America, which is an unprecedented injustice. Because you will not get anything for the marvellous artistic pleasure that I have enjoyed through your works, may I with due modesty herewith enclose my contribution.

The letter included a five-dollar bill.

These five dollars—then worth little more than £1 sterling—didn't signify much to Sibelius, except that he was touched by the friendly attitude of the man! But some decades earlier they would probably have been as a gift from heaven in his everlasting struggle against poverty. That Sibelius was generally able to get by was due to several small bequests that came to him from childless relations, otherwise he mostly lived on bills of exchange. As he himself told me, in his worst period he was involved with something like sixty such bills. Every time the rent or some larger sum was due Sibelius went to the bank to discount a fresh bill. This nearly always worked—which was apparently due to his eminent name and captivating personality, but surely also to the support of his many friends. In his early years good and bad criticisms clearly influenced his financial affairs. Lack of success in the concert room could completely cut him off from credit for a time.

In spite of all difficulties Sibelius took care punctually to attend to his bills and honestly to his other obligations. But it was unavoidable that from time to time the pressure on him was very great. He was not even spared the ignominy of a visit by the

Justices' debt officer at the time when he was being honoured by the whole nation.

After the great celebrations in honour of his fiftieth birthday the representative of the debt office came to Ainola and stuck his stamp on the new Steinway grand which Sibelius had had as a present from a group of admirers. What was owed was paid off with the greatest expedition and Sibelius had the piano until his death. However, Providence decreed that his lot should be easier than that of many other great composers. He lived a long time and did not have to die in want, as did Mozart, Beethoven and Schubert. Every year his situation improved—particularly after the setting up of agencies in the different European countries for the protection of royalties in respect of music. These, observed Sibelius, 'were almost too good to be true'. In the last decades of his life he was well off, wanting nothing.

Old people who are distinguished generally consider that money matters are somewhat disreputable, and Sibelius was no exception. 'If one can give a person nothing but money the sum at all events should be large,' was his attitude more or less. Mrs Sibelius used to affirm: 'He was certainly not stingy with the housekeeping money. Even when we were most poor if only he had money he made provision for me without any nagging. Somehow or other he always got it in the end.'

One day when she was once more talking about the same subject Sibelius, looking waggish, suddenly asked: 'What would you have said if I had become mean in old age?'

Then the three of us burst out laughing. The thought was too comic to admit of any other reaction.

In my small way I was frequently aware of the open-handed nature of my famous employer. As an old man he had nothing more to do with money matters, leaving them all to his wife. But he always paid my salary himself, at the same time dealing with my expenses in respect of postage, telegrams and various purchases, for which he categorically refused to accept any account. At the beginning I tried to make clear what I had spent—at least in respect of major items—but he didn't want to know. He only asked for the total amount, and then always paid more than I had asked.

Payment was always made most discreetly, when there was no one else present.

From time to time I marvelled at the excellent memory of the old master. Not once in twenty years did he ever forget my account. Once indeed I did think that this had happened. He had asked me what he owed me, and, as he usually did, went to his room to fetch the money. Precisely at that moment Mrs Sibelius came into the library and spoke to me about something I was to attend to. Sibelius heard us, came back, and joined in our conversation. This went on a fairly long time and then we attended to some letters. But scarcely had his wife left the room than he took the money from his pocket and handed it to me across the table. His eyes had a playful expression, for he had read my thoughts and was amused at the surprise he had given me.

SEVEN

Sibelius and the great masters

When I paid my first visit to Sibelius he said to me with some emphasis: 'I would particularly like to make it plain that I never talk about my own activities as a composer.'

I told him that I took that for granted since in general I was not capable of talking with him about such matters, my music studies having been of a very modest order. I had spent some years in the orchestral class of the Conservatory, where I mostly played the violin. But when I came to Ainola what I had learned in the way of theory I had long since forgotten, while now I hardly ever played the violin. All that I could in fact offer was my love for music. So how could I have been in a position to talk to the great composer about his vocation?

Courteous as ever, Sibelius hastened to assure me that he had not meant that. He would speak with no one about his creative work. I was soon able to establish that in this respect he was entirely consistent. 'It is,' he would say, 'a closed book.' In the course of the years I used to have to answer many questions, both in writing and by word of mouth, by saying that the master never made any comment about his own music.

This total silence had several causes, of which two in particular seemed to me to be entirely understandable. Sibelius often told me how infinitely difficult it was for him to clothe his ideas about music and art in words. The true nature of music, in his opinion, stood far removed from all mundane things. He said:

> The older I grow the more difficult I find it to say anything about the art. Superficial tittle-tattle about music seems to me just as if someone amid all the row and crowd of a *palais de*

danse were to ask his partner: 'Do you believe in the existence of God?'

Sibelius never said anything about the second reason for his resolution, but I could easily guess at it. It was a consequence of the 'Silence of Järvenpää', that everybody was aware of; the fact that he had not published anything for years. He didn't want to say a word about that and therefore simply declared that he wouldn't talk to anyone about his music.

In this delicate situation I naturally considered the master's wishes. Accordingly I never asked any questions unless he gave me opportunity. But in the course of time it was unavoidable that we should often get to talking about music and art. Gradually his resolution grew weaker and weaker so that in later years he spoke quite freely to me, even about his own works. I learned his views about music and art and even about the nature of his own creativity. We often talked too about his relationship to other composers. Modern music and the future of music interested him particularly, and this was a theme to which he often returned.

To the best of my ability I tried to make a precise note of his remarks, since I knew how little he had otherwise said about such matters. What he had to say was seldom in detail, let alone exhaustive, for he was much too lively and impatient. For the most part he let himself go in aphorisms—with no more than a few sentences at a time. But for Sibelius that was a lot. Like a good stylist, who quite instinctively limits himself to what is essential, he always hit the nail on the head.

The relationship of a composer to his predecessors is always of considerable significance to the composer himself, and so I made a note of everything that Sibelius had to say about the great masters. As was the case with every other composer, Johann Sebastian Bach was his incomparable exemplar. This was so when he was young, when—as he himself was wont to say—he played the violin sonatas 'with indifferent success'. He said less about Bach than about other composers because, as was obvious, the stature of the great master of the baroque was taken for granted. He was only to be admired, and expressions of opinion and alternative points of view were superfluous. Sibelius wanted performances of Bach's works that were simple and unaffected, for he was too monumental to be interpreted subjectively. He who would perform Bach should forget himself.

Sibelius received many letters requesting that he should compose now this, now that. A lady singer once asked him whether he had not thought about writing church music. Sibelius made me reply that it always seemed to him that to compose sacred music in the light of Bach's mighty life-work was quite pointless.

In an exhibition of old instruments in Berlin he one day saw a harpsichord that had belonged to J. S. Bach. It was fitted with two manuals, like an organ. Because it was already late in the afternoon Sibelius decided to wait until closing time. Then, after everyone had gone, he gave the attendant a tip and asked if he could play on Bach's harpsichord. 'I almost had a sense of something that was holy,' he told me with eyes ablaze.

While the great Thomascantor so clearly had first place in his affections it was not very easy to allot the second place. Did he prefer Mozart or Beethoven? I would say that he admired Beethoven but loved Mozart. He regarded the latter as the greatest master of orchestration, and several times told me how the G minor Symphony had run through his life like a red thread. 'The Finale,' he said, 'is especially marvellous. I would like to hear that at the time of my death.' He also talked more than once about another of Mozart's works in the key of G minor—the string quintet (K. 516). Helmuth Thierfelder,[1] remembering a phrase of Sibelius, said that it was pretty clear that Mozart was his favourite composer: 'There is nothing in the world more beautiful than the Mozart of the G minor Symphony!'

One gloomy February day after I had just arrived in the large room at Ainola a few rays of the sun penetrated the clouds. The brightness lasted only for a brief moment. Then it became dark once more, but a feeble glimmer of light remained on the lower edge of the clouds. After Sibelius had greeted me he went to the window and looked at the sky. He said: 'That reminds me very

[1] Dr Helmuth Thierfelder, German conductor and leader of the Municipal Symphonic Orchestra, Hanover.

much of a Mozart *Adagio*. When Mozart takes his farewell of a theme there is always something that is melancholy—particularly in the *Adagios*. The character of this sky for me is like such an *Adagio*.'

In general he spoke to me a great deal more about Mozart than about Beethoven. This can certainly be attributed to the fact that he was well aware of my admiration for Mozart. I would adduce as significant, however, the answer he once gave me when one day we were discussing the developments that had taken place in the world during the last century.

'And what about music?' I asked. 'Does that only go forward?'

Sibelius considered for a moment.

'That is a question that is not at all easy to answer,' he replied thoughtfully. 'Its development is not that of visible nature.'

He stayed silent for a while and then, slowly and reflectively, said: 'To a certain extent, however, Mozart has more of the Christ figure than Bach and the other great composers who preceded him.'

I was surprised that in this connection he mentioned Mozart rather than Beethoven, which is what most musicians would have done. I still believed at that time that after Bach Beethoven was the greatest figure in the history of music so far as Sibelius was concerned, for as a composer he certainly had a closer relationship with Beethoven than with Mozart. He always said that he himself had followed the 'compulsive' policy of Beethoven. In relation to musical history one could perhaps say that Beethoven was the first Romantic and Sibelius the last. But neither was solely a Romantic; both stood on the watershed between two great musical epochs.

Sibelius admired more than anything in Beethoven the inflexible determination to create, and the moral depth of his works. 'It is inconceivable that they don't appreciate Beethoven's greatness,' he once expostulated, all put out when having read a superficial piece by some young modernist. 'Beethoven's works have many failings, especially from the period of his total deafness. But they live.'

At the beginning of 1951 an English editor invited Sibelius to write his interpretation of Beethoven for an intended symposium. Such requests were almost always declined on the grounds that the master would only make public his thoughts through his music. But on this occasion Sibelius had read an interesting article by Wilhelm Furtwängler, and he told me to reply that the famous conductor had precisely expressed what he himself would have wished to say about Beethoven.

In his essay 'Beethoven, a world force', Furtwängler wrote:

> What is most evident in respect of Beethoven and exerts more influence than anything from other composers is what I would term the 'Law'. He strives like no one else after the natural law, and after what is definitive, as a consequence of which we have the extraordinary clarity that distinguishes his music. The kind of simplicity that prevails therein is not the simplicity of naïveté, nor is it a calculated effect like that, for instance, of a modern popular number. Yet at no time was music written that confronts the listener so directly, so openly and—one might say—so nakedly! We know from Beethoven's life that he never found his work as an artist easy, that the monumental and simple qualities of his themes did not simply fall into his lap. On the contrary: each of his works shows a concentrated essence of a whole world, and—from a limitless, chaotic life and experience—is given order, form, and clarity by means of the iron will of the artist. This particular kind of clarity signifies nevertheless the renunciation of all means—which exist in art as in life—of placing the subject in an advantageous light so that through kinds of colouring and through refinement it may appear as more profound and greater than it really is.

In reading these words of Furtwängler one instinctively thinks of Sibelius's own works, most of all those of the later period, from the Fourth Symphony on. It is not surprising that he felt Furtwängler's statement to have been his own.

Sibelius once visited the State Library—then known as the Royal Library—in Berlin, and there he saw the original score of the Ninth Symphony of Beethoven. 'It was full of cancellations and alterations,' he said. 'At first glance one could see that it was a matter of life and death, a contest with God.'

That seemed to please Sibelius. His eyes shone as he spoke

of Beethoven's gigantic struggle. He was obviously thinking of his own life's work and found satisfaction in the knowledge that he alone did not have to bear the labour-pains of a great musician.

In the summer of 1954 he gave me a small book about Beethoven that had interested him. This was called *Beethoven and the French Revolution*, in which the author (a Catholic bishop) [1] wrote about Beethoven's revolutionary views. At times—as is well known— these were very radical, and Prince von Metternich was always having occasion to wrinkle his brows at the composer's indiscretions. The actual theme of the book was not one likely to enthral Sibelius, who had no taste for social revolutionary views. But Bishop Noli had described Beethoven's human weaknesses and living habits in detail, and Sibelius discussed them with me at unusual length. I had the impression that it gave him some satisfaction to compare himself with that musical giant, the account of whose personal characteristics afforded Sibelius a greater understanding of him.

In a Concert Guide that someone once sent to Ainola the works of Sibelius were described as programmatic and at the same time compared with those of Beethoven. Sibelius found this description fundamentally inaccurate. He said:

> One could have said of Beethoven—if one absolutely insists— that he wrote programmatic music. For his point of departure was always a specific idea, whereas I . . .

The sentence broke off. Sibelius noticed that he had trodden on dangerous ground, and changed the subject. Perhaps his sixth sense had conveyed to him how my heart beat faster when I thought that I was on the point of hearing an important statement about his work from his own lips.

So far as Brahms, his wife's favourite composer, was concerned, he regarded him as an epigone of Beethoven, a fact that was bound to reduce Brahms's significance in his eyes. In any case he did not appreciate him in the same way that he appreciated Mozart and Beethoven—not to speak of Bach. He once said to me that Brahms

[1] Bishop F. S. Noli, Mus.B., Ph.D., *Beethoven and the French Revolution*, New York, 1947.

became clearer in old age—from which is to be understood that in his youth Brahms had seemed to lack clarity.

The well-known singer Ida Ekman wrote to Sibelius shortly before her death and told him how she had met Brahms in Vienna at the house of Eduard Hanslick, the music critic, and had sung one of Sibelius's songs for him. This was *S'en har jag ej frågat mera* (*For I have asked no more*, Op. 17, no. 1). This pleased Brahms so much that he wanted to hear it again, and he took Hanslick's place at the piano. When they had finished he kissed the young singer on the forehead, saying: 'When we next meet you must sing more Sibelius than Brahms.'

Next day it so happened that in the street and quite by chance Brahms met his Finnish friend Filip Forster—a teacher of singing at the Conservatory in Vienna. He immediately hastened to tell him about the Sibelius song, which can be appreciated as a considerable tribute to the young composer. Brahms did not very often show enthusiasm for the works of his contemporaries, and it was only when he came across true talent that he was prepared to support the claims of young musicians.

Ida Ekman's letter gave Sibelius a lot of pleasure, for he was delighted that Brahms had enjoyed his song. His papers could be in an indescribable disorder but he was always able to find this letter, which he often showed to me, and certainly also to a lot of other people. All in all it was easy to see that in the final reckoning he very much admired Brahms.

As a young man he had wanted to study with Brahms. When he went to Vienna in the autumn of 1900 he took with him a letter of recommendation from Ferruccio Busoni to Brahms. But Brahms no longer took pupils. He was well to do and as a bachelor spent practically nothing, so why should he have to put up with pupils? 'Is he any good?' he asked. He did in fact get to hear that the young Finn had written a good string quartet, but that didn't alter his determination at all.

Sibelius in fact seldom had anything to say about Brahms and even less about his contemporary and rival Anton Bruckner, although he had very decided views about his music. I never heard him say a derogatory word about Bruckner. 'Why, why all that!' he

expostulated when we talked about how poor Bruckner was persecuted and cat-called. Sibelius fully understood the deeply religious
quality in Bruckner and was moved by the humility of the 'musician
of God', though at times he was amused by his helplessness.

There was one anecdote which he often told to his guests.
During a rehearsal a conductor had asked Bruckner whether in
one place in the score the note should be F or F sharp. With a deep
obeisance Bruckner replied: 'That is entirely as the maestro
himself wishes.' Sibelius preferred to hear Bruckner's symphonies
in their original form, without any abbreviation. He said, 'They
have been absolutely falsified, just as Rimsky-Korsakov falsified
Mussorgsky.'

Richard Wagner—who was so warmly admired by Bruckner—
was the one among the great German composers who had the least
appeal for Sibelius. A number of musicologists are of the opinion
that like many other late nineteenth-century composers Sibelius
as a young man felt oppressed by the greatness of Wagner.
Tristan und Isolde particularly is supposed to have had a very
strong influence on him. But from what Sibelius said to me the
'Wagner complex' can hardly be taken seriously and in any case
he got over it very quickly. In the summer of 1894 he visited
Bayreuth twice when *Parsifal*, *Tannhäuser* and *Lohengrin* were
performed. He was never there again. The performances were outstanding and *Tannhäuser* was conducted by none other than
Richard Strauss. The theatre was filled with admirers of Wagner
from all over the world. But Sibelius himself did not feel any particularly close affinity with Wagner's art. He enjoyed *Parsifal* best,
but the almost ecstatic admiration with which the really devout
Wagnerians approached the music of the master seemed to him
positively grotesque. 'It was,' he said, 'as if they had taken
Holy Communion.' The whole town was full of Wagner souvenirs.
On the driver's seat of one of the carriages that were for hire he
once saw the word 'historic', which was meant to signify that
Wagner had used it once or twice.

After the Festival Sibelius went to Munich, where he heard
several Wagner operas and made a thorough study of the scores.
But neither then nor later could he really reconcile himself to

Wagner's music. In the 1930s he once said to the composer Bengt de Törne, who was a pupil of his at the time, 'Wagner is coarse, brutal and vulgar. Refinement of feeling quite eludes him.' De Törne made this opinion public and caused a lot of indignation among Wagner fans. Sibelius got agitated protests and once even an impertinent and quite shameless letter—which went straight into the wastepaper-basket. He had, of course, not intended his remark for publication. When we once spoke about it again, he said, 'Wagner indeed was a genius. In *Tristan*, for instance, he had a theme that was altogether magnificent.'

However, that was the only time I heard him praise Wagner. About the second significant Romantic, Franz Liszt, he never spoke one word. That may seem strange when one considers that Sibelius himself had written a series of symphonic poems. Between him and Wagner (and also between Sibelius and Liszt) there was a fundamental difference. Wagner meant his music to serve a complete work of art and thus provided it with a specific programme, which was never the case with Sibelius. So far as he was concerned, the topic—as, for instance, a ballad from the Finnish national epic—was never more than a point of departure for his inspiration. This stimulus aroused in him a state of mind, a mood, from which the music came forth without constraint. In this sense then his symphonic poems are to be defined as absolute music, and under these circumstances it is understandable that he considered the artistic means of Wagner altogether too artificial and often almost banal.

While Sibelius had little understanding of the later Romantics the earlier representatives of this school meant a great deal to him. As a child and in countless chamber music evenings he had got to know them well. As he told me, at that time he was completely captivated by the Romantics and this predilection lasted all his life. From innumerable remarks I was able to appreciate how important they were for him. He interpreted the Romantic idea in the widest sense; in fact, according to him, almost all music more or less belonged to this category. 'Romanticism is the innermost essence of music,' he once said as we were engaged in a discussion of modernism.

What is Romantic is imperishable. It always has been, and always will be, as long as people inhabit the earth. It is only the kind of species labelled 'intellectual', that exists today, that can doubt this. We human beings need much more than the kind of reality that is accessible to the five senses. He who does not understand that fact is unfortunate.

Of the earlier Romantic composers Chopin meant least to Sibelius, and I find nothing at all about him in my notes. Sibelius was no pianist and when he was young Chopin's few chamber works, one supposes, were seldom played. Perhaps the Slavonic-French character of Chopin was somewhat alien to him.

The great German Romantics, Schubert, Schumann and Mendelssohn, meant much more to him. We talked about Schumann a good deal in the autumn of 1952 after I had published a biography of Robert and Clara. Sibelius, friendly as ever, praised the book and kept on coming back to Schumann's life and works. Above all he admired the inexhaustible sense of poetry, particularly in those works in which Schumann's lyrical talent was most fully expressed. Regarding the four symphonies he had this to say:

> Construction was not his strongest side. And so far as orchestration is concerned there is a certain degree of helplessness. He believed that by doubling with two different instruments [that is, both playing the same notes] he could produce a stronger *forte*. In fact it produces the opposite effect.

In December 1949 the Robert Schumann Society in Zwickau (Schumann's birth-place) elected Sibelius a member of the artistic committee and a little later an honorary member of the society. In his letter of thanks Sibelius related how he had played a great deal of Schumann when he was young, and in February 1889 had even been the second violin player in a Helsinki performance of the E flat quintet. The pianist was no less than Ferruccio Busoni, who was at that time a teacher in the Conservatory of Music in Helsinki and a close friend of Sibelius.

It may seem remarkable that Sibelius had the highest regard for the works of Felix Mendelssohn. It is now almost the fashion to regard Mendelssohn as somewhat out-of-date and sentimental.

But Sibelius was of another opinion. I never heard him say anything unfavourable about Mendelssohn; on the contrary he was often full of praise. Sometimes what he said was surprising. 'After Bach,' he observed as one day we were talking about the Cantor of St Thomas's, 'Mendelssohn was the greatest master of fugue. It sounds strange, maybe, but nevertheless it's true.' He often stated that in the history of music there were only three child prodigies—Mozart, Mendelssohn and Saint-Saëns—of whom the last never in the end attained the stature of the other two. According to Sibelius Mozart and Mendelssohn were the two greatest masters of orchestration. One day he showed me an English article that he had received. He was irritated by it, saying:

> The author attacks me because of my opinion that even today Mozart and Mendelssohn are unrivalled in respect of orchestration. He mentions Stravinsky, Shostakovitch, and other modern composers. How little understanding is there, thinking in terms of history. Mozart and Mendelssohn did not use the instruments of today. What would they not have achieved if they had lived now!

Mendelssohn's violin concerto in E minor certainly had something to do with arousing Sibelius's admiration for the composer. Sibelius having wished to become a violinist had intensively studied the concerto with a view to public performance. But I believe that the essential reasons lay deeper. The musical language of Mendelssohn found an echo in the Finnish master's heart.

Sibelius used to like to tell his visitors a true story about Mendelssohn's Trio in D minor. When he was once a guest of Alexander Siloti in St Petersburg, Eugene Ysaÿe, Werschbilowitsch, the unforgettable Russian cellist, and Siloti, were to play this Trio. The result was truly astonishing. Each of the three virtuosi listened only to his own instrument, and they completely wrecked the work. 'That,' said Sibelius straight to the leader, 'is terrible!' The music gave way to general laughter.

I sometimes used to hear Sibelius praise long-forgotten composers of the era of Schumann and Mendelssohn. I remember that he very much enjoyed the songs of Robert Franz. 'Why doesn't anyone sing them any more?' he asked. 'Robert Franz has written the loveliest things.'

Of the later Romantics—among whom he himself had his place —Sibelius certainly liked Edvard Grieg the best. The esteem in which he held Tchaikovsky in his youth, and of which there are certain traces in his First Symphony, significantly diminished in later years. But all through his life Grieg was in his opinion a great Nordic tone-poet. When Grieg celebrated his sixtieth birthday towards the end of 1903 Sibelius sent his cordial good wishes, in return for which he received an equally cordial letter of thanks. He treasured this letter from Grieg as a precious memento. He showed it to me in the autumn of 1949, telling me at the same time that he had learned from Ida Ekman of Grieg's high regard for his compositions. She told him: 'You can hardly have a more sincere admirer than Edvard Grieg,' And this pleased Sibelius very much.

In the autumn of 1942 Sibelius was asked for a statement on the occasion of the Grieg centenary. He was never pleased to get such requests, but on this occasion he dictated the following message to me:

> My gratitude for what Edvard Grieg, Norway's great son, has given me in his music is only to be compared with the warm admiration I entertain for his art.

I heard less about Antonin Dvořák, the Czech composer, than I did about Grieg. In 1901 Sibelius paid a visit to Prague and then made the acquaintance of Dvořák. This introduction was effected by Dvořák's son-in-law, Josef Suk, who had been in Helsinki with the Bohemian String Quartet shortly before this. Dvořák was then sixty years old and at the peak of his fame. 'He was,' said Sibelius, 'a delightful man, his whole nature warm and friendly, and I shall never forget his clear blue eyes. He remarked that he had composed too much music.'

Of the composers of the Romantic epoch who had some significance for Sibelius I ought not to leave unnoted Johann Strauss, the king of waltz and operetta. Sibelius admired him very much, as also did Mendelssohn, Brahms, Liszt and Wagner.

Sibelius never talked about the music of his famous contemporary Richard Strauss, which was partly to be explained by the fact that Strauss's music did not interest me very much. On the other hand he frequently used to speak about Strauss the man, and always with gratitude and appreciation. He had much to thank the German composer for. The Heidelberg performance of the *Kalevala* Legends had been of the greatest importance for him and Strauss also championed his works on later occasions. There is no doubt that Strauss for his part had a high regard for his Nordic contemporary. He once spoke quite honestly to an American conductor on this point: 'I can do more, but he is the greater.'

In conclusion, I will say something about Karl Goldmark. Certainly he was not among the great composers, but Sibelius was his pupil when he studied in Vienna in the winter of 1890–1. At that time Goldmark was very well esteemed and he was busy in many directions. He did not, therefore, have much time to give to pupils. It was a long time before he would see Sibelius at all, but finally he said he was prepared to receive him. 'I like to help young artists,' he said, which made Sibelius more than happy. Until then no one had called him an artist; he had only been a music student.

The assistance consisted of Goldmark going through the works which Sibelius composed at home, with suggestions for improvements and alterations. He had no time to give systematic instruction, so Sibelius at the same time studied with Robert Fuchs— 'Serenade Fuchs' as the Viennese called him.

At the start he wrote an overture for orchestra which, full of hope, he took along to the great man. Goldmark read the manuscript through, and with no beating about the bush said that it was no orchestral work but chamber music arranged for orchestral instruments. Sibelius thereupon wrote a second overture, which his strict master found much more to his liking. In general pupil and teacher got on well together.

Only once was Goldmark in a really bad mood—but the reason had nothing to do with music. He had a young and very pretty niece living with him. In order to reach his teacher's study Sibelius had to go through the drawing-room. One day he met the niece in the drawing-room and in his courteous way passed the time of day with her. Almost every young woman immediately took a fancy to Sibelius, and this was also to be the case with Goldmark's niece. At any rate she was always in the room when the Finnish student came for his lesson. But this was not to be permitted for long. One day Goldmark came into the drawing-room by chance, and his features at once took on a heavy scowl! He was bad-tempered for the whole hour and this time found nothing good to say of his pupil's work.

From that day on Sibelius was never allowed to go into the drawing-room, but had to use another entrance. He had seen Goldmark's beautiful niece for the last time!

EIGHT

⋙⋙⋙⋙⋙⋙⋙⋙⋙⋙⋙⋙⋙⋙⋙⋙⋙⋙⋙⋙⋙⋙⋙⋙⋙⋙⋙⋙⋙⋙

Modern music

What was Sibelius's attitude to the new music, to the modernists of our time, and to all the upheavals that have taken place during this century?

I must make it clear at once that, as in all other respects, his views were very positive. For one who was so old Sibelius must be regarded as exceptional. New ideas always evoke a reaction, and at first have more opponents than supporters. Many people take it as a personal affront when something appears with which they cannot make contact. How easy it is to dispose of all new music as 'nothing but a load of rubbish' or, at best, as empty searching after effect. The works of Robert Schumann in his own time were considered by certain critics to belong to the class of 'so-called unintelligible music'; Bruckner composed 'dreadful cacophony!' while an amusing book has been compiled from the countless abusive remarks about Wagner and his works.

Such a negative, not to say hostile, attitude was entirely out of keeping with the character of Sibelius. A warm feeling for all that lives and strives on this earth was a necessity for him. It was impossible for him not to judge the new music affirmatively and with complete confidence in the young composers. 'It matters a good deal to them that we don't doubt the integrity of their efforts,' he said to me more than once. The new tendencies in music and its development aroused in him a strong interest, and in this respect too he kept his intellectual vitality right to the end.

One can justly ask how, in his isolation in Järvenpää, Sibelius managed to familiarize himself with modern music. Naturally he

1943 : Sibelius on a summer walk at Järvenpää.

Aino Sibelius in 1944.

The composer's home, Villa Ainola.

Villa Ainola, seen from the main road.

Part of the library at Villa Ainola.

The composer aged seventy-nine.

View from the drawing-room through the dining-room.

Voces intimae. Portrait taken in 1949 at Ainola by Yousuf Karsh, Ottawa. Reproduced by permission of the photographer.

The composer in 1954, aged eighty-nine.

The last photograph, taken in 1955, two years before Sibelius's death.

knew well the senior moderns—Hindemith, Schoenberg and
Stravinsky—for he had frequently heard their works when he was
abroad. With more recent music he was kept in touch by means of
ra lio and recordings, while he often got scores from young composers. Being cut off from living music in this way is not unimportant, for it is precisely contemporary compositions that lose
much in radio transmission. Certainly Sibelius had a first-class
receiver which was a present and always kept in the best condition.
He heard much modern music, principally—but not exclusively—
from the Swedish radio. He would often sit by his radio until late
into the night.

There was one composer in particular among the senior
moderns whom Sibelius esteemed; that was the Hungarian Béla
Bartók. If the conversation ever turned to him Sibelius was always
full of praise. To the best of my knowledge he never met Bartók,
but he was well acquainted with his music. 'Bartók was a great
genius, but he died in poverty in America. I don't know what he
thought about my music, but I always had the highest regard for his.'

He did not use terms of praise for other modern composers. He
regarded Paul Hindemith as a distinguished craftsman. He said:
'First and foremost he is a German artisan—very clever, but
lacking in compulsion.' Hindemith's works reminded him of
Albrecht Dürer's copper engravings and woodcuts. He told
Hindemith this in October 1955, when Hindemith paid a visit to
Finland to receive the Sibelius Prize.[1] Hindemith was somewhat
taken aback, and Sibelius hastened to assure him that he meant
what he said as a compliment.

I had the impression that Sibelius held Hindemith in higher
esteem than Schoenberg or Stravinsky. One evening in the autumn
of 1947 when we were talking about the future of music he said:
'When I think of Hindemith I have the feeling that a composer of
genius will come one day and will follow Hindemith's lead.' This
sentence meant in fact that he attributed a mission to the German
composer in the history of music, although he did not count him

[1] The international Sibelius Prize was founded by Antti Wihuri, the
ship-owner and philanthropist in 1953 for outstanding composers. It is
worth 70,000 Finnish marks. The holders of the Prize up to date are
Sibelius, Hindemith, Shostakovitch, Stravinsky and Benjamin Britten.

among those creative artists who are impelled by some inner force. Once he expressed his astonishment that Hindemith denied every inspiration. It was Sibelius, however, whom Hindemith had to thank for his Sibelius Prize.

He also complained that Stravinsky undervalued inspiration. He didn't particularly enjoy Stravinsky's music although he was ready to acknowledge his artistic integrity. But he found it somewhat disquieting that he had gone through many different stylistic periods, and that even in recent years mixed styles were to be discovered in Stravinsky's works.

Sibelius, of course, knew Arnold Schoenberg's dodecaphonic system well, although he himself never made use of it. He could not share the admiration of present-day young people for Schoenberg, but he paid due respect in his own independent way. 'I was,' he recounted, 'one of the first to get hold of Arnold Schoenberg's works for himself. I bought them on Busoni's advice, to learn something. But I learned nothing.'

How could a composer like Sibelius, finding inspiration a necessity for all his creative activity, have understood the constructive manner of Schoenberg's functioning? In the opinion of Sibelius the form of a work was the necessary consequence of the musical content. A kind of music that was tied to a strictly ordained series could have for him no interest other than technical. He also believed that of all modernists Schoenberg was the one in whose works a preponderance of technique was most evident.

'Alban Berg is Schoenberg's best achievement,' he once joked. He had just been listening with much interest to a radio performance of one of Berg's works. Up to a point, therefore, he put Berg at the head of the Schoenberg school. But it was not long before he gave it as his opinion that Berg's significance as a creative composer would be transient.

I once asked Sibelius if he had ever felt like introducing quartertones into his music. He answered at once: 'No, never. That's the kind of experiment that is forever being made—and forgotten in next to no time.'

When a journalist visited him in the autumn of 1951 he expressed himself more plainly still: 'I can't stand Alois Haba: it sounds

all wrong to my ears. Schoenberg somehow or other I can digest.'
Of the senior modernists then it was really only Béla Bartók who
was regarded highly by Sibelius, and he always enjoyed hearing
Bartók's music. In later years the others of this group did not
particularly interest him. He already knew them so well that he
could not alter his opinion.

That did not mean that their followers were all the same so far as
he was concerned. Indeed, their efforts were of great interest to
him. Even in old age he wished to be well informed as to what was
going on in the world of music, for it was precisely what was then
taking place that he considered of the greatest significance. He said
to me with some vigour, 'The present epoch is one of the most
important in the history of music.'

What did Sibelius intend when he said this? Was it that among
the young composers he had discovered outstanding creative
abilities? Unfortunately that was not the case. He mentioned from
time to time that he had heard a work which was interesting, and it
seemed that he considered some composer talented. But he never
found a really big talent. I had the impression that he was looking
for a composer who had what he considered the prime requirement
for every viable work of art: a powerful inner impulse. But it was
just this that was lacking in the young composers with whom he
was acquainted.

He talked to me a good deal about this, particularly in his later
years.

> It is fantastic how much one can do today. The young have
> every prerequisite to develop their skills. Radio, records,
> pocket scores and modern methods make learning easy. In my
> time we had to go to Paris to hear Berlioz's *Fantastic Symphony*.
> Today one only has to stretch out one's hand. And yet truly
> there are few real composers. It is difficult to let go of a first-
> class technique especially when the inner content is weak. The
> artist easily identifies himself with his technical skills. How
> endless a lot of well-composed music is—but nothing else than
> note-scribbling. The inner life is absent. They've built a huge
> shipyard—but where is the ship?

Once he said of a certain composer in jest: 'He is an outstanding
musician—like everyone today.'

Sibelius never criticized modern music on account of its radicalism, which he seemed to feel was entirely natural. I cannot say that it pleased him. 'It sounds so dreadfully ugly,' he once sighed from the very depths of his soul. But his criticism was never directed at external things. He was quite clear that there must be development in everything, and always asserted how short-sighted it was—in music as in all else—to cling to the past.

I remember how he spoke to me about this one evening in Ainola. We were in the ante-room and I had already said goodbye.

'There's an entirely new era coming,' he said. 'Not only in the material but also in the spiritual field. At night when I'm not sleeping I have a strange but clear feeling that everything becomes new.' I went out and the door shut behind me. But Sibelius opened it again and concluded: 'In music too.'

How did Sibelius feel about modern music as a phenomenon of this development that he took to be essential? At the beginning of 1953—when he was already in the habit of speaking to me with complete freedom—we talked about the matter in detail. He said:

> The main thing with today's composers is cerebration. What they write is more mathematics than music—sometimes even only mathematics. It is serious that it is often devoid of inner life. I can't imagine that the music of the future can be so contrived as that of today. It is inconceivable that ethics are entirely missing in what is written now. In the end these are the foundations of every valid art. But I can't believe that music will always be as it is now. What is written today is often no more than empty sound effects which are completely superfluous if the composer himself has anything to say—and that is all that matters. Personality can show itself in five notes. What is eternal sometimes lives in very modest form.

I particularly noted that he spoke of 'five notes' and not 'several' as one might have expected. This means that he used five-note sequences.

Often I observed the sympathy he felt for a young composer who sent works to him.

'What a long and endless way this poor young man still has to travel,' he said one evening as we sat in the library. He was turning the pages of a score, while I was reading letters. 'One can see from this work that he himself is very enthusiastic, and yet it counts for nothing.'

'All the same, how can one see his enthusiasm?' I asked in some surprise, even though I was already aware of the sixth sense.

'One can do that,' Sibelius replied with a laugh, 'when one has been composing music oneself for sixty years.'

But—even with the best will in the world, which Sibelius assuredly possessed—he could find nothing more than technique in the works of the majority of young composers. How, in spite of this, was he able to declare that the present was one of the most important epochs in the history of music?

> Not all periods are marked by creative character. There are periods of preparation and transition, and those are also necessary. Stamitz and the Mannheimers shaped the forms which were later used by Haydn, Mozart and Beethoven. It is not absolutely necessary that anyone who produces something new should himself be a great creative genius. For after him come others who breathe spirit into his forms. The time in which we live is just such a period of transition, and, indeed, one that is more important than any earlier period. What modern composers do has a far-reaching significance. The most part of the modern music that I have heard will not survive, but the young composers are preparing the way. One can rightly say of them, 'They who have given satisfaction in their own day have made a contribution to all ages.'

With these words of Hans von Bülow, Sibelius also expressed his belief in the future. He seemed to think, then, that the new golden age of music could be near. I recall how in conversation one evening he was very passionate:

> Sometime a great genius will appear, who will unify all that today we term 'modern music'. Who knows, perhaps he is living among us, hungry in a draughty attic.

In December 1948, just before his 83rd birthday, the Finnish Radio invited him to give an interview. The interviewer came to Ainola, and Sibelius, sitting in his easy chair in the library, answered his questions off the cuff. The last question was: 'What advice would you like to give, Professor, to a young composer?' Without a moment's consideration he replied: 'Never write a superfluous note. Every note must be experienced.' Discussing this a few days later, Sibelius added: 'I would also have liked to say: each note must live.'

Sibelius seldom named names when he said anything about the young but often talked of whole groups. The Russians interested him very much, which in part was probably due to the fact that in Järvenpää reception of the Soviet radio was excellent. At the beginning of 1945 he said:

> There is a great deal of fertility coming from Russia. Shosta-kovitch is in talent very like Richard Strauss was, and committed to the time in which he lives. Recently I heard his Seventh Symphony, which I take to be his best.

Sibelius enjoyed a high reputation among the musicians of the Soviet Union, and this they liked to demonstrate. The Association of Soviet Composers never forgot to send him greetings on his birthday.

Sibelius had a very special sympathy for the musicians of his own country. For a full half-century his tremendous form had put a whole generation of composers in the shade. The appearance of an internationally acknowledged genius in the modest circumstances of Finland was an event of such consequence that all other efforts in the field of music necessarily seemed very minor. It was not easy in Finland to appear as a composer when every endeavour was immediately compared with the work of the great master, which was ever increasing in significance.

Sibelius was well aware of all that. If he had not otherwise come to understand it, he would have sensed it through the jealousies that are generally to be found in the neighbourhood of famous people.

But envious people would have been surprised if they had known how tactful and sensitive Sibelius was in respect of his Finnish colleagues. He never needed publicly to pass judgment, for he never functioned as a critic and indeed had no disposition towards criticism. He was too good-natured for that function. If ever the name of a Finnish composer was brought to his notice he always had something friendly to say. That was a basic principle, but it was also rather more—an inner reaction. As I was able to establish on a number of occasions he was depressed because, without his wishing to do so, he had hindered the efforts of other composers. Because of that he wanted to help them, and in that he was very consistent. He was concerned even about the Swedish composers, among whom he had a number of friends. I once showed him a programme prospectus in which there was an announcement of the symphony concerts of the Stockholm Symphony Orchestra for the coming season. It contained three of Sibelius's Symphonies, the violin concerto, and *Tapiola*.

'I am played a lot there,' he said, but his voice did not sound particularly cheerful. 'Swedish composers must be peeved that my works are permanently in the programmes. The fight for places there is a hard one, and their own works are very seldom performed.'

In twenty years I could all in all note down only two observations unfavourable to Finnish composers. The one slipped out by mistake in answer to a reflection of mine. At the time there were just the two of us in the room and we were talking about a composer of the older generation.

'I like his music quite well,' I said. 'But I have the feeling nonetheless that something is lacking.'

'The spark,' Sibelius answered.

But then he was dismayed at what he had said and jerked himself up in his chair so that his cigar nearly fell out of his hand.

Speaking with some force he said, 'You can't tell anybody that. It must remain strictly between us.'

So I will never reveal who it was about whom Sibelius then spoke, nor to whom his second remark referred. In expression this was quite different, but in content very similar.

We were listening to a radio concert, of music that was conventional, without interest or personality. After the transmission had ended the rest of us—Mrs Sibelius at all events was in the room and perhaps someone else—waited in silence in case the master wanted to say something. He noticed this and didn't want to disappoint us.

'Beautiful music!' But he spoke so despondently that no one could doubt what he really thought.

NINE

The creative artist

'Music is on a higher plane than everything else in this world.' I would like to quote these words of his as a motto, as I now relate what Sibelius told me, across the years, about his own work as a composer and his relationship to music in general.

In the climate of intellectualism in which we live people readily regard artistic creation in exactly the same way as any other mental activity. I knew a young engineer—a clever, competent man—who proposed in all seriousness that it was theoretically possible for anyone to develop into a second Sibelius if he could only have sufficient time. Somewhat modestly, however, he opined that a lifetime would probably be insufficient for the purpose.

Sibelius's view of the creative function of the artist was a very long way from that of the engineer's philosophy. For Sibelius composition was a vocation, to some extent a message from a higher sphere. 'It is,' he said, 'brought to life by means of the *Logos*, the divine in art. That is the only thing that really has significance; yet it is impossible to explain it through words.'

From time to time Sibelius sought indirectly to define this eternal germ of composition, for which there is no intelligible description. It was the innermost essence of music. It determined the difference between a work of art and a useless labour, but it could appear in stronger or weaker form. The ethical striving of man and his aspiration to God were closely linked with this eternal germ. Consequently it was absent from music that was constructed intellectually or was merely mechanical. It was the most important prerequisite for a truly symphonic work. The composer himself experienced it as an inner compulsion, and Sibelius spoke about it a great deal.

It is, incidentally, to be noted that Sibelius certainly was not the only great composer who felt that his work was divinely inspired. It can almost be said that every single composer who created anything of real, lasting value considered himself as a tool in the hand of God. Haydn, Mozart, Beethoven and Brahms said words to that effect. Beethoven wrote about his mission: 'There is nothing higher than to approach nearer to the Godhead than other men, and from here to diffuse the rays of the Godhead among mankind.' The cheerful Haydn did not take the matter so solemnly. But he put on his best clothes when he settled down to compose. 'I will now converse with God and so must be suitably dressed,' he said. Shortly before his death Brahms told the American musical writer Arthur Abell in detail how he experienced divine inspiration. He said: 'All true inspiration comes from God. There is no great composer who has ever been an atheist, and there never will be.' Wagner, Richard Strauss, Edvard Grieg and many others have expressed themselves in the same vein. Speaking of his world-famous opera *Madame Butterfly*, Giacomo Puccini said, 'God dictated this music to me.'

Sibelius liked to use the expression 'the compulsion', which he had from Beethoven. Sometimes he also spoke of an inner urge and an inner necessity, or simply of the desire to create. Across the years I was able to conclude that the compulsion, as Sibelius understood it, was a very comprehensive idea. Inspiration as it is usually understood was only a part of it. Generally speaking one does not associate compulsion with artistic inspiration. This is merely a condition which makes it easier to work and which, in consequence, leads to better results.

According to Sibelius the compulsive element was much more; it was not only a servant but frequently and exactly a master to whom the artist had to submit himself. It was not always enjoyable. 'The most unfortunate people,' he said, 'are composers for whom their work is an inner urge. I am just such an unfortunate composer.'

Mrs Sibelius frequently talked to me about her husband's

creative compulsion. Always when a great work was in process of composition Sibelius lived as though in a trance, which reached its climax when the work was being written down. Nothing could then hold him back from composition. His brother-in-law Armas Järnefelt used to complain when he had to leave some cheerful social gathering in order to finish a work. Every hindrance was painful to Sibelius, and he was miserable if the urge seized him and he was not able to work.

Such a state could perhaps be described as an extraordinarily strong inspiration, if it were not that the sense of compulsion—as Sibelius explained to me—resolved itself in work. Thus it not only spurred the composer to work, but at the same time directed his creative ideas and feelings and controlled his frame of mind, from all of which the work derived. Sibelius talked a great deal about this kind of urgency which determined the content of a composition.

I once wrote a biographical article about Anton Bruckner, and before doing so I read a number of source works. In the course of my reading a moving sentence which the 'musician of God' used more than once caught my eye. 'I could indeed compose in another manner, but what would the dear God say about it?' Soon afterwards I went to Ainola and I recounted Bruckner's words to the master. His face lit up and he exclaimed: 'So you see, Bruckner knew exactly what the urge to compose was.'

Sibelius always said that he composed instinctively, never deliberately. This instinct of the creative artist was obviously the imaginative force through which the inner urge shaped the work. Since the form and content of a composition are closely linked together it is evident that the form had to be under the control of the inner impulse. For Sibelius music that was written according to formula was not a work of art. In music of that kind everything that to him was most important was missing. 'Thousands of such works have been written,' he said, 'and they have all been forgotten. It is often thought that the essence of symphony lies in its form, but this is certainly not the case. The content is always the primary factor, while form is secondary, the music itself determining its outer form. If sonata form has anything that is lasting it must come from within. When I consider how musical forms are established I frequently think about the ice-ferns which, according to eternal laws, the frost makes into the most beautiful patterns.'

The problem of form and content often appeared to exercise Sibelius's mind a great deal. Perhaps this was due in part to the fact that, mostly at the beginning of his career, the formal structure of his own symphonies was often criticized. He said:

> My God! In the course of my life I have got to hear more than enough on that score. Furtwängler even once remarked in all seriousness that I was no symphonist at all, but an Impressionist. I used to say in response to this kind of comment: 'What are your forms to me?' This is nothing to do with form: it has to do with life and death.

His works are the best proof that he knew precisely what he was talking about. At first they gave such an impression of originality that their form also caused astonishment. Later research has made it clear that Sibelius's symphonies, created—as he himself said—instinctively, demonstrated the form of the classical symphony with remarkable exactitude. The Seventh, which apparently has no division into movements, in this respect is often held up as no more and no less than a model for students. Sibelius himself was frequently surprised when he read articles on his works. He used to say: 'When a work of art which is intuitively created is scientifically analysed it reveals amazing requirements. Yet the artist works entirely instinctively.'

I once asked him why he had revised several of his works. He told me in this connection that in respect of almost every major work he had to fight a severe battle so that he could shape it exactly in accordance with his inner commands: 'My symphonies were a terrible struggle. But now they are as they must be.'

He firmly believed that he had fulfilled what his artistic conscience demanded of him. 'Even great composers,' he declared, 'have had to make sacrifices to the taste of their time. But only those works in which the composer has remained absolutely true to himself can last beyond their time.'

We once spoke about the future of his music. His opinion was:

Very likely I shall have my own place. Composers have their
periods. For a time, maybe, little notice will be taken of my
works, but I believe that I can hope that they will not be
completely forgotten. In every true work of art there is a spark
that can never entirely be extinguished.

Above all Sibelius was a symphonic composer, which is clearly
shown from his own observations on music. The territory that was
most properly his was that of absolute music. Even in his symphonic poems—of which he wrote a whole series—he surrendered
himself to the frame of mind that the particular subject evoked.
The work then formed itself freely from out of the artistic instinct
and never on the foundation of a precise programme or conscious
description. But if his music contained moods of nature of an
astonishingly vivid quality, that is to be explained by the strong
insights of the composer and the striking force of his musical
language.

Sibelius always particularly wished to emphasize that all his
seven symphonies were pure, absolute music, and exclusively
fashioned from his own musical ideas. They had no programme
element at all—although many people say that they have—and all
the thematic material was his own.

For foreigners Sibelius for many years was a typical nationalist
composer. *Finlandia* certainly had a lot to do with this, but people
of other countries were impressed by the strange, Finnish character
of his musical language. Very early it was spread around that he
had made use of Finnish folk-songs in his works. In old age
Sibelius fought a hopeless battle against this fallacy. That his
music should have taken in anything from outside was an intoler-
able idea to him.

Some musicologists believe that they have proved that the
master's music has certain points of contact with Finnish folk-
music. In my opinion—for what that is worth—that could be
correct. What I believe is that while Sibelius never consciously
made use of folk-song, it is possible, if indeed not probable, that at
some time—probably in the earliest years of childhood—folk-
music was firmly planted in his subconscious, to be blended with
his own music later on.

But that was not the reasoning in the many letters and articles that, to his annoyance, again and again came to Sibelius's notice. Even today one can read essays about Sibelius in which it is stated in all seriousness that his music is principally based on Finnish folk-melody. With a sigh Sibelius would say, 'These stories about folk-melodies have pursued me all through my life,' and as soon as he read an observation of this kind he got me to write a rebuttal. There were a whole lot of fans, who otherwise would scarcely have received answers to their letters, who had Finnish folk-song to thank for the fact that Sibelius sent them messages signed by his own hand. Provoked by so much error in commentaries on his works, in his later years Sibelius sought altogether too eagerly to deny the national element in them. His music breathed the spirit of the Finnish character, he declared, but he was not to be classified as a national composer in the same sense as, for example, Smetana or Grieg. That was quite right and proper.

By the side of the large-scale orchestral works his other compositions—songs, piano pieces and choral works—meant a great deal less to him. They were thought of as under the shadow of the principal works, and outside Finland very seldom performed. However, Sibelius believed in their future, and was never inclined to consider them merely as insignificant *pièces d'occasion*. Even the songs and piano pieces, he stated, represented his innermost self. His views on the suitability of poems to set to music were interesting. They should first of all be of such a nature, he suggested, that they could be elevated to become works of art through music. They could then inspire a composer. When a poem was perfect in itself it had no further need of music.

The ideas within a text appeared to Sibelius as a fairly subordinate issue, being so far as he was concerned no more than material on which to work. He said: 'My songs can also be sung without words. They are not so dependent on poetry as the songs of many other composers.' He regarded them also as definitive in form, and not to be tampered with. At the beginning of 1946 he told me he had forbidden the Finnish Broadcasting Company to perform his songs other than in their original form, with piano accompaniment. 'I don't want them orchestrated,' he said, 'for they completely lose their individual character. One can't express little ideas by means of a large orchestra.'

Nevertheless from time to time when someone wished to orchestrate one of his songs he gave his consent, because for some reason or other he didn't want to refuse the request. Mostly this was entirely the result of his kindness. In earlier years he even made a number of orchestral arrangements himself when asked to do so. Most often these were for Ida Ekman, who was incomparable in performing the songs.

Sibelius wrote a large number of his best songs for Ida Ekman, who was always suggesting that he should do something new. He once told me that the *Flower Songs* (Op. 88) had been written for a limited vocal range, because at that time, in 1916, Ida Ekman's voice was rather restricted in compass. For his part he inspired the singer to the highest endeavours, and she told me herself that when Sibelius was in the audience she sang as if upheld by a magical influence. She always received his songs at the last moment, although he had promised them weeks, if not months, beforehand. For example, the programme had already been printed for a long time when she got her first sight of the first three songs of Op. 26— *Svarta rosor* (Black roses), *Men min fågel märks dock icke* (*But my bird is long in homing*), and *Bollspelet vid Trianon* (*Tennis at Trianon*). One of his most beautiful songs, Op. 38, *På verandan vid havet* (*On a Balcony by the Sea*), was brought by Sibelius, all out of breath, to the railway station when Ida Ekman, waiting for him with a pulsing heart as she counted the minutes, was about to start a recital tour.

On a Balcony by the Sea was one of Sibelius's own favourite songs. Once when we had played a record of Marian Anderson he told me that he had long hoped that the great Negro singer might sing this particular song, and that her accompanist of many years, the Finnish pianist Kosti Vehanen, had obviously had something to do with it.

One evening Sibelius mentioned quite in passing that he had composed songs only during a very brief period of his life and that afterwards he had lost interest in this activity. But very soon he repented of this remark. Early next morning—much earlier than he normally got up—my telephone rang and Sibelius again took up our conversation of the previous day. 'During the night I was annoyed about what I said about my songs,' he said, and added that he didn't at all wish to describe his songs as insignificant, but that he considered both his vocal and his piano pieces as well up to standard.

Up to now very little notice had been taken of the piano pieces, but that could not convince the composer that they were unimportant. On the contrary their limited popularity aroused in him an aggressiveness that was rarely evident. 'I know that they have some future,' he said, 'although today they are almost entirely forgotten.' We had been talking about Robert Schumann, and Sibelius added that one day perhaps his piano pieces would be just as popular as those of Schumann. He never spoke in this way about his orchestral works, which in his later years brought him only praise and gratitude. Scarcely a day passed on which the symphonies or the tone-poems did not continue on their triumphal progress somewhere or other in the world. This is why the comparatively few observations I had from Sibelius about his own compositions related principally to his orchestral music, which was by far his greatest interest. When he was young he considered chamber music the noblest form of music, but later on symphony took first place in his scale of values.

Once Sibelius observed in passing that what was written about musical ideas could significantly increase the composer's productivity. 'Unused motivs are as golden grains in later years,' he said. I would have liked to have heard more on this subject, but, as was so often the case, Sibelius would not answer questions directly. To my surprise, however, he said, 'Each of my seven symphonies has its own style, and their creation in every case took a lot of time. But I never talk about my own work; for next morning I would regret having done so.' This comment was supplemented by another which I noted down somewhat later: 'One can get the ideas for a symphony very quickly.'

At this juncture I refer to what Karl Flodin, a well-known music critic, once wrote just after the Third Symphony had had its first performance:

Is there another modern symphonist who thinks so orches-
trally as Sibelius? He dreams horns, breathes divided violins,
goes to bed and wakens up with clarinets. The whole of his life
and being is music. He once told me how an old painted wall of
a house immediately transformed itself into music. The
'painted wall motiv' formed itself in his imagination in a
moment. He must have hundreds of such motivs of which he
remains aware from year to year. When the creative spirit is
awakened, he takes motivs from their hiding-place according
to the requirements of the compositional process at the time.

Flodin certainly did not invent this observation, but must have
heard it from Sibelius himself. But in later years Sibelius never
again spoke so openly or in such detail.

He once said that he wrote his music down when he first heard
it in its final form in his mind. Between the first conception and
committal to paper a long time—sometimes years—passed. A
work thus came to maturity, at the same time acquiring its own
style.

Here it should be mentioned that Sibelius did not often approve
of theories put forward about the origins of his themes. Cecil Gray
and a number of other musicologists after him have remarked that
Sibelius first stated his thematic ideas in fragments, so as to
assemble them into actual themes later on. When that was under
discussion between us in the autumn of 1950 Sibelius quite
categorically said: 'That's not true at all. I do not build my themes
out of small fragments.' I would have liked to hear what he
himself had to say about the origin of his themes, but as usual he
would not go into that.

When Sibelius said that he inwardly heard a work a long time
before it was written down he meant much more than other
composers who have said the same thing. That is to say he heard
his music already in instrumental form. The majority of composers first write a short score and only deal with orchestration
afterwards. Sibelius never did that, but wrote directly into full
score bar by bar.

I once asked him if he often had to think about which particular instrument should be considered. Without hesitation he
answered: 'Never! My music is ready in its instrumental form.

Actual "orchestration" is something with which I am quite unfamiliar. I let the musical ideas develop of their own accord.'

This independence of ideas in this connection means no more than that the instrumentation of his music was also determined by an inner urge. I was, however, most surprised when he told me that he had even heard all the instruments of the orchestra in his imagination when he was a child: 'When I then heard an actual instrument for the first time I recognized it at once, and right from the start we were old friends.'

Sibelius had no use for new instruments: 'I can say everything I want to say with those that are available today. One must only understand how to use them properly.' He spoke several times about percussion instruments in contemporary music.

> We take them from primitive people, whose treatment of them is much more assured than ours. The significance of these instruments is much greater than people in general believe. Their time has now arrived. Drums are extremely important in the orchestra, and the drummer must be very musical—which is understood only by a very few.

In his youth Sibelius almost hated the woodwind, because it was always then out of tune. Either the instruments or the players were bad—mostly both. The result in any case was always entirely other than the composer had intended. In a letter Sibelius mentioned that in one place in his Sixth Symphony he had written *ppp* for the bassoon, although he knew quite well that it was impossible for the player. He only wanted the bassoonist to play as softly as was possible. In that way Sibelius got a somewhat stronger *mp*, which was what he had wished for. In the same letter he mentioned similar places in other of his scores.

It was of the greatest importance to him that his works should be properly performed. If he heard a faulty performance on the radio he would grumble about it for days afterwards. Unfortunately this often happened. 'It is inconceivable how unfamiliar my works continually are to present-day conductors,' he wrote to Georg Schnéevoigt. This was as late as 1942 when he had long been world famous. Particularly in countries where his music was beginning to take root, the *tempi* were always wrong. It could happen that a young conductor would take sections twice as slowly as he should have done, but mostly *tempi* were too fast. Sibelius, referring to this, often said that the unrest of the technological age communicated itself to music.

> Composers and conductors of today generally don't seem to know how a real *Adagio* should sound. It becomes increasingly clear to me that it must be very hard properly to perform my symphonies. I didn't previously understand that.

He did what he could—conductors got carefully composed letters from him: every word was weighed in the balance so as not to offend the recipient. He often asked his publisher if he would put in metronome markings for the benefit of the ill-informed conductor. But that he only did as an emergency measure and without expecting too much from it. 'One can't put everything into notes,' he said. 'A great conductor gets inside the work and feels the innermost endeavours of the composer. He must be able to read between the notes. If anyone doesn't understand that, metronome marks won't help him much.'

On occasion Sibelius lost his nerve altogether. After a deplorable radio performance of a work—I don't now recall which it was—he even got the extraordinary idea that the conductor had done it badly on purpose, because the man for some reason or other grudged him any success.

Even though there were a great number of them Sibelius was always critical of recordings of his works. One evening when this was being discussed, he sighed as he said: 'Actually I have never been completely satisfied with any single recording.'

TEN

⊳⊳⊳

The silence of Järvenpää

The musical world waited for thirty years in vain for a new work from Sibelius. After the last great creative period, which produced two symphonies and the tone-poem *Tapiola*, there was nothing but silence, except for a few small unimportant pieces for violin and piano, until the master's death.

Why was it that Sibelius composed no more? I had to give an answer to this question countless times, and always said that I had no idea—although that was not entirely true. But it was simpler that way. In this chapter I will indicate what I learned concerning the matter with the passage of years.

Sibelius often used to say that we men easily forgot the lessons of the past. Taking this particular comment of the composer into account one could properly ask how Sibelius could have written fresh masterpieces in old age. When he wrote *Tapiola* he was sixty, and in musical history there are only very few great symphonists who have composed works of significance in their seventies. Haydn and Bruckner are the great exceptions, but Beethoven wrote his Ninth Symphony at the age of fifty-three, the same age as was Brahms when he wrote his Fourth. When he wrote his last important works—the clarinet sonatas—he was also sixty. Mozart and the Romantics all died relatively young.

In the general sense, then, Sibelius was no exception, but rather the rule. Reduction of creativity in the sixties is a general pheno-menon, but one which applies particularly to artists dependent on their inspiration.

It is wrong, however, to assume that Sibelius did not compose any more after he was sixty. So far as he himself was concerned it would have been much easier if he had not bothered. In 1926 an inner struggle began which only ended shortly before his death. The evening of the master's life would have been far happier without this struggle.

When I became Sibelius's secretary I knew, as the rest of the world knew, that for nine years he had published nothing. But he told me that in spite of this he did still compose. Although he otherwise kept silent in seven languages on the subject of his work, he always assured me that he still went on with it. To publish and to compose were two quite different things, he said. Several years later he said, 'I am always composing,' and he approved my publishing that remark in my little book, *Jean Sibelius and his home*, which appeared in 1945.

I thought then that in all probability Sibelius referred to the inner originating process—i.e. the planning and maturing processes, that precede the writing down. At no time did I see a manuscript, and if by chance there had been one he must every time have hidden it well away before I came on the scene.

For years he never gave me any inkling of what he was writing, although he again and again asserted that he was continuing to work. One day as we were discussing his dreams he told me how in his sleep he often conducted two movements of a new symphony. He added that these two movements were always absolutely clear.

'And are they clear later, when you are awake?' I asked, although I thought he was too clever to walk into this trap. I got no direct answer but, to my surprise, he said: 'I have many sketches for my Eighth Symphony.'

The Eighth Symphony, then, was the cause of his constant struggle. That he seemed to have precisely two movements complete in his dreams is easy to understand; for it is generally believed in musical circles that he had virtually composed the first (?) two movements of the symphony as early as 1927—that is, soon after *Tapiola*. But in August 1945 he told me that he had destroyed the whole work. 'My Eighth Symphony,' he said, 'has already been "ready"—"ready" in inverted commas—several times. I even went so far as to put it in the fire.'

Some days later he wrote a letter to Basil Cameron in London and repeated the same words almost exactly—but with the last sentence deleted. Another time, later on, we spoke about the burning of the Eighth Symphony. I suppose that after that nothing more that was 'ready' remained on paper. In the summer of 1949 he informed an acquaintance in California that he would leave no new work behind.

I believe that in his old age Sibelius had no other work than the Eighth Symphony in mind. There is only a single observation to suggest the contrary. In March 1945, when it was obvious that the war was coming to an end, we spoke of how Finland was now cut off from the whole world. The Eighth Symphony was mentioned at the same time.

'When it is ready,' I observed, 'we shall have re-established contacts with abroad.'

'Is it necessary now that it should be a symphony?' asked Sibelius quietly.

I got the impression that he did not mean anything in particular, but it is not impossible that at that time perhaps he did have something else than the Symphony in his thoughts.

I often heard remarks which at most quite clearly, and at least in all probability, referred to the Eighth Symphony. It was always cropping up in correspondence. Whenever he was asked to compose something—which happened not infrequently—he made me reply that he was attached to the idea of a bigger work. He made use of this expression on many occasions, and often said to me that he would complete a major work before his death.

In the early years he seemed to be sanguine that he would succeed in doing so and even later on he would not admit anything to the contrary. In the autumn of 1949 he emphatically said to me: 'I'm certain that I shall write a work before I die. When that will be, I don't know, but I know that I shall write it.'

Next winter—by now he was eighty-four—he had a letter from a musician inquiring if the numbering of the catalogue of works, ending with Op. 116, was applicable still.

'Do we need say more than that later opus numbers are not available?' I asked.

'Not yet available,' Sibelius stressed.

Even as late as the summer of 1953 he told me in the course of a wide-ranging discussion that he was still in fact working on the new symphony. But at that time his faith was not so strong. 'I have the new Symphony in my head, but who knows what will become of it. But it lives and I concern myself with it a great deal during the hours of night.'

He always liked to talk about the fact that he was composing, not only with me but also with his many visitors. In his letters I was never permitted to use turns of phrase that might have implied that his work was already completed. Any sentence giving such an impression was deleted. Once I had written: '. . . Because Professor Sibelius doesn't any longer write songs.' The old master would not let that stand. 'Certainly I will compose more songs,' he said quite calmly, '—at the right time.'

He always said to his guests: 'Yes, indeed, I am composing, even though I haven't published anything for a long time.' He used that sentence frequently. A reporter from the American magazine *Life* once tried to speak to Sibelius in bad German—since I had told him that that was Sibelius's best foreign language. 'Es wird schon kommen,' Sibelius said to the reporter, who probably hoped to learn something more about the mysterious Eighth Symphony.

When I was first with him I sometimes asked myself in private why Sibelius kept on insisting that he was still composing. But— as we had agreed right at the start—I never asked him. Gradually it became clear to me that it was a matter of psychological complex, the dimensions of which I only understood much later. He worried that he was no longer able to compose. Other great composers were fortunate in that they died at the height of their powers; but Sibelius had thirty years of inner strife, the hopelessness of which he must have recognized early on. But not for anything would he suggest that his life's work had reached its end—that, so to speak, he was a living corpse. But he also tried to deceive himself, and that was the worst thing of all. If he could have come to terms with his circumstances his old age would have been far more harmonious.

The two of us were strolling in the garden one warm summer evening and Sibelius looked as though he were particularly enjoying the sublime quietude of nature. Suddenly he said: 'A summer evening like this banishes all cares. In the presence of nature I always feel a sense of liberation.'

In jest I responded, 'Why cares? What kind of cares can a world celebrity have?'

'We all have our share, but I must have had much more than most to straighten out.'

'I can't understand that at all. Anyone who has great achievements behind him has the right to enjoy his old age in peace and quiet.'

I saw his eyes light up for a brief moment, but his smile was sad. Nothing could compensate for loss of the only joy that had ever really signified anything to him—that of creation.

Every artist has critical periods in which he is not able to work. Sometimes they can last long. Times like these are the most difficult of his life, and occasion deep depressions which extinguish faith in his own capability and seem to render all effort meaningless. But such periods of transition can at the same time lead to heightened awareness and to a kind of transfiguration, and the return of pleasure in creative activity more than makes up for the troubles of a period of difficulty.

For thirty years Sibelius hoped that he would be able to compose again; but this particular joy never returned. The 'long silence' altogether engendered in him a kind of feeling of guilt, which I was often able to observe. He found it very hard not to be able to do what was expected of him. It might have been easier had he not been in receipt of a generous allowance from the State. Year by year this also increasingly bothered him, particularly since when he was younger he had accepted bursaries and subsidies as a painful duty.

He took it very hard when from time to time newspapers commented on his long silence. He would remark with some bitterness: 'When a composer has not brought anything out for a long time they say that he can't do anything any more and is finished. One can struggle for years with one work.' The postman had just brought an American paper with a blunt article about the 'Silence of Järvenpää'.

His fans all over the world unwittingly also gave him a lot of worry, for every other letter ended by saying that people were awaiting a new masterpiece from him. There were many who believed in the rumour that Sibelius had a pile of unpublished works in his desk. And there were always inquiries from publishers. A naïve American publisher once asked for nothing more than a piano concerto and a violin concerto—both in a short time. Another publisher was so tactful as to invite Sibelius to write a 'Children's Symphony' in the style of Haydn, as if to say that the old master could perhaps manage that.

There were also many really important proposals, which did him great honour. In the autumn of 1949 the Royal Philharmonic Society asked Sibelius if he would write a new work for the Festival of Britain in 1951. He replied that he could not promise anything definite, and there was no further inquiry. Only a few months later, in January 1950, the American National Theater and Academy wished for an overture for the celebration of the 150th anniversary of Washington D.C. Inquiries such as these always reminded the master of his misfortune. Business-like requests were courteously answered in the negative, others not infrequently with a few humorous comments. Once, for instance, he wrote: 'I have so often promised to write a piano concerto that I wouldn't like to trouble my conscience further.' But mostly he replied briefly, that he was occupied with a major work—which was indeed correct.

This major work, the unborn Eighth Symphony, continually haunted the correspondence. Many inquiries about it came and they were seldom easy to answer. Two famous orchestras had secured the right to a first performance—the Royal Philharmonic Society in London to the world premiere, the Leipzig Gewandhaus Orchestra for the first performance in Germany. In July 1939 Sibelius reported to Leipzig that the Symphony was not yet 'ready for the printer'. A month later, in reply to a further inquiry, he said that not enough progress had been made for a first performance to be considered for January 1940, as the Committee had proposed.

The association with the Royal Philharmonic was of earlier date, going back indeed before my time. At the beginning of February 1940, in the gloomiest days of our 'Winter War', they asked from London if the Symphony could be played in a concert in aid of the Finnish Red Cross. It must have been bitter for the master, particularly on this occasion, to have to answer that he had nothing to offer.

It was clear that the Royal Philharmonic Society shared the universally held opinion that the Symphony had been ready for a long time, but that the composer would not have it performed before his death. Rumours of the utmost variety concerning the work were in circulation, and they were quickly disseminated by the world's press. Immediately these caused a stream of letters and newspaper cuttings. When this happened it was always hard for the old man. Sometimes he was awake the whole night and was very depressed. He also had visitors to look after by day when, if they spoke enthusiastically about the Eighth Symphony, he had to put on a sunny smile.

In his last years Sibelius had to weigh practically every word so as not to start rumours. Once we drafted a letter to Shura Cherkassky, the American pianist, who not long before had been in Finland, without Sibelius, however, having been able to receive him, for some reason or other. Sibelius dictated: 'You wouldn't have had much pleasure in my company anyway. For I am actually reading proofs and anything more boring I can't imagine.' Hardly had I reached home when the telephone rang and Sibelius asked me to say in the letter that it was proofs of his youthful works he had been reading. 'Otherwise,' he said, 'they'll again think that the Eighth Symphony will be published.'

Before any red-letter day in the composer's life the ghostly symphony always came to life in the press. A week before his seventieth birthday *The Times* bluntly wrote as follows:

> Those who have visited the composer tell us that he has the Symphony in his head. It can only be of benefit to the world, however, when it is on paper. Although we can understand Sibelius's wish to live out his old age in peace, we would, nevertheless, like to hope that he would once more show himself able to respond to the good wishes of his admirers by means of a concentration of his musical ideas.

Shortly before Sibelius's eightieth birthday Cecil Gray sent a telegram asking whether it was true that the Eighth Symphony would now at last appear. The telegram reached Helsinki late at night and the telegraph office sent it not to Järvenpää but direct to my flat. Hardly had I read it than I realized that I would now have to cause the master some annoyance. After all the preparations for the great day he was exhausted, and I would have preferred to say nothing. But I could not do that, since the inquiry came from a man of such importance. So next morning I telephoned Sibelius.

His voice was bright and cheerful, but it changed in a moment as soon as I had read him the telegram.

'This unfortunate Symphony once more,' he groaned. 'I can't think about it any more. We won't answer.'

He hung up, and I considered what I should do. Cecil Gray was the author of the first English biography of Sibelius, and an earnest admirer and champion of his music, who had boldly proclaimed the greatness of the Finnish master. It just was not possible to ignore him. He would with justice have felt deeply offended. For the first and last time in twenty years I decided to go against the express wishes of Sibelius. I sent a telegram to London, reading: 'Regret Eighth Symphony not yet available. Hearty greetings. Sibelius.'

The master never learned of this missive. I had thought that Cecil Gray would write a letter. I would then have sought absolution and certainly would have received it, with a few kind words into the bargain. But apart from a message of congratulation there was no further letter, and in the turmoil of the great celebrations Sibelius forgot the whole matter. It was not mentioned again.

But Sibelius could not forget the Eighth Symphony. It pressed heavily on his mind, and the world at large took pains that gossip about its non-appearance never ceased. Letters were always coming in which the sensitive question was raised—either after beating about the bush or straight out. As time went on they got so much on Sibelius's nerves that he did not answer them. 'This everlasting chatter puts me right out of humour,' he said with some irritation.

At the time of his ninetieth birthday Mrs Sibelius and I decided that as far as possible we would not show him inquiries of this kind. The correspondence by then had grown so large that for a long time Sibelius had not himself been able to read all the letters. That was my duty, and I referred to him only the most important matters. However, he often caught me out through his 'sixth sense'. Scarcely had I glanced at a letter and discovered therein a reference to the unborn Symphony, than quite contrary to his normal practice he would ask with a slight sense of disquiet what was in the letter. 'Only a fan, who doesn't want anything special,' I would answer, throwing the letter on the large pile in which in the last years so many letters unfortunately were entombed.

But it was not only letters and people who had been to see him, who referred to the silence of Jävenpää, that put the old man into a dark mood. In his own home everything reminded him of the sore point. In the drawing-room there was the great piano; in the library the record-player; while from his windows he could all the time see the glories of nature which had been so much involved in his creative work.

Then there were the quite insignificant things that awakened associations with his creative days. One hot summer afternoon I drew the blind over the window because the sun was shining straight in my eyes. Sibelius immediately pricked up his ears. 'It's strange how my heart used to beat faster when I heard that noise,' he said. 'I used to do that countless times when I was composing. It gave me a remarkable sensation here.'

He laid his hand on his heart and stayed motionless for a while, as if he had inwardly recalled the happy days of long ago.

New works by older composers also often made him sad. He was always most warm in congratulation and in wishing them continuing creative capacity. But it was not difficult to guess that there was a thorn in his own heart. 'You who are more than fortunate . . .' he wrote to his friend of many years, the artist Louis Sparre, who had produced one of his great works in old age.

It was very moving how in his troubled state Sibelius would spare a thought for someone else. Purely out of friendship he used to ask if I had done any photography of late. He knew how much pleasure the camera gave me. When I once told him that I hadn't had any time to use my camera for almost half a year he immediately commiserated with me. 'Has my asking that upset you?' he inquired sympathetically.

It was just as though in some way it had become possible to compare my little hobby with the tragedy of the Eighth Symphony.

The silence of the great composer after he was sixty would probably not have created much of a sensation if it had not been for *Tapiola*, of which the first performance took place in New York in December 1926, conducted by Walter Damrosch.

As a creative achievement *Tapiola* differs hardly at all from the rest of the tone-poems, but it aroused astonishment that immediately after this work came total silence. In 1929 Sibelius published a few small pieces for violin and piano (Ops. 115 and 116), but thereafter nothing more. People asked themselves how it was that a great composer should produce a masterpiece at the end of a rich creative period and then suddenly become forever silent, as though he were dead. If *Tapiola* had showed significant weaknesses then the 'silence of Järvenpää' would have been more easily understood. But what had happened?

Some critics certainly thought that they had discovered such weaknesses, even immediately after the first performance in New York. One remarked that certain signs pointed to the drying up of the artistic imagination of the composer, and it was only at the end of the work that he thought he found passages that reminded him that a great master from the north had once given voice to an incomparable musical language. Even Olin Downes, the tireless American champion, was dissatisfied at first. In his opinion *Tapiola* as a whole was not so convincing as most of Sibelius's earlier orchestral works.

Against this, however, there are quite contrary assessments to be cited. No one would dispute the technical mastery of *Tapiola*, and a large body of expert opinion considered that the tone-poem should in fact be placed among Sibelius's most important works. Cecil Gray said that this last work alone would have guaranteed Sibelius a place among the greatest composers of all time even if he had written nothing else.

It was small wonder that the whole world asked itself why the composer did not compose any more. As I have already remarked this question was wrongly put. After *Tapiola* he composed precisely that work which the world was waiting for from him—the Eighth Symphony. But why did he deny it? And why had he to remain silent for thirty years?

Aino Sibelius, who was nearer to the composer than anyone else, answered this question in two words: rigorous self-criticism. The master himself once said something along these lines: 'Heaven on earth begins when man forsakes self-criticism.' He said this without particular reference, and to some extent as an exposition of his own thoughts.

In earlier days too he had been severe in judging his work. The same was true of most of the great composers who preceded him—among others Johannes Brahms, who destroyed about half of his works. In May 1949 Sibelius told me more or less the same thing about himself: that he had published only half of what he had written. He did not say that he had destroyed everything else, but in any case he left behind no unpublished works. In museums and in private possessions a large number of juvenilia are to be found, but he was hardly referring to these. I believe that the Eighth Symphony was not the only work which Sibelius destroyed. This is supported by another of his statements: 'If I had published everything that I had written, the catalogue of my works would have been a great deal longer—in the region of 180 Op. numbers.'

He spoke again and again about the unpublished works of his youth, with evident disquiet. He was oppressed by the thought that after his death they would be taken out of their hiding-place and made public.

> I would much prefer to have them all back, but there are far too many for that. I don't remember most of them any more. I don't know them by name, but I recognize them when I see or hear them. When they were written there was, as we now understand the term, no musical public in Finland. Those who were enthusiasts made a really exclusive circle in which everyone knew everyone else, and I was often asked to conjure up something for this or that occasion. So I strewed about me a vast number of occasional things that now give me no peace of

mind. One is always turning up somewhere. When I wake up
in the night and think about it I am thoroughly depressed.

He wrote to the Director of the Sibelius Museum in Turku
several times about youthful pieces which were in the museum.
He always said that they should never be performed or published,
'not even after my death'. He got a very nasty shock in the autumn
of 1950 when the museum wanted to broadcast a performance of a
trio from 1888 in honour of his eighty-fifth birthday. At first he
intended telephoning the museum director immediately to prevent
the mischief. But then he changed his mind because he was aware
of his own weakness. 'They can get round me,' he said. 'They will
say that the trio has already been rehearsed, or something. It
would be better to write a plain no.'

I never got to the point of following up this matter and would
not ask Sibelius about it afterwards. In later years especially I
avoided everything that bothered him. For a long time it had
become clear to me that the way he worried about his early works
was part of the same complex as the Eighth Symphony and the
'long silence'.

Taking everything into consideration one can hardly doubt that
a self-criticism that increased year by year was one of the reasons
that caused Sibelius's silence. Once he wanted to write to one of
his publishers: 'If I can offer anything which I know for certain
you will accept . . .' On my advice he removed the sentence, but he
said to me: 'I wouldn't like to make such a fool of myself that my
composition could be returned to me.'

The question now is whether this self-criticism was justified or,
as Mrs Sibelius believed, unreasonable. For my part I favoured
the first alternative. Particularly in the last years, when Sibelius
spoke to me with great freedom, my opinion in this respect
hardened. To my mind there was no reason to believe that he did
not precisely know what he was doing, and it was not for nothing
that he burned his last symphony. It was only the frame of mind
that the unborn work aroused in him that was unreasonable. 'Am
I really a great composer?' he could ask in all seriousness.

The longer he lived and the more he experienced changes in the
world around him the greater his difficulties grew. The hideous-

ness of the Second World War took away from him any inner peace. In February 1943 he said to me, 'I labour at a great work and would like to finish it before my death. But the inhumanity of this war makes my work the more difficult. I can't sleep at night if I think about it.' In the autumn of 1945 he spoke to me again in this manner, saying that what was happening around him made it difficult to work. He used in this connection the saying *tempora mutantur*, etc.; he was well versed in Latin and not infrequently made use of classical expressions.

Sibelius was disturbed also by the new tendencies in music. When he was young and inspired by the compulsive urge to create he had not unduly concerned himself with what was happening around him. But after years of silence he had to appreciate that amidst all that was new and changed he represented a period long since forgotten. His interest in modern music pointed to this, since he always came back to the point that technical skill had developed so immeasurably.

A great deal of significance should also be attached to the purely external disturbances with which Sibelius had to contend. As soon as he had written his First Symphony he looked for a quiet place in the country, and his need for peace in which to work increased year by year. But for a man who was world-famous there was no more peace. Early in 1951 he said to me:

> I am composing a new symphony, but who knows if it can ever be written down. So much goes on around me that upsets me and hinders me. I can't concentrate. And my family is now so large that I can't go into retreat. There is always something important or something worrying happening.

In that he was indeed correct. He was like Abraham. All his five daughters were married and there was a great tribe of children, grandchildren, and great-grandchildren. Practically never were they all in good health at the same time. It was as the master himself said: 'I have so many descendants that I am always learning that one of them is running a temperature of 40 degrees.' Then there were deaths which supervened, to make work impossible for a long time.

But the worries that came from outside the home and the family were much worse. Year by year the correspondence grew, and every morning there were great piles of letters, journals and parcels. Not even a completely full-time secretary could have prevented more and more important problems turning up with which the master himself had to deal. Articles containing the most astonishing observations and errors were not exactly the thing to help his peace of mind.

There was never any lack of visitors. It was only in his very last years that the old man was effectively protected from them. It was no wonder that he was not able to work when sometimes he had to entertain an important visitor on every day of the week. Not infrequently there were two visits on the same day. For an artist a distraction of this kind is much worse than for other people, because after the guest has departed he cannot without more ado sit down and bury himself in his work.

Finally, Sibelius had a physical infirmity that made it very difficult for him to work—that is, to write. In later years his hands trembled a great deal, particularly when, as was frequent, he was in a nervous or depressed state. 'I wrote a letter to Tali Paul [1] myself yesterday,' he told me in the autumn of 1954. 'It was a terrible job. And yet I hope I can still compose.'

Sibelius had all these difficulties against him. Nevertheless I would say that in the final issue they were of secondary significance; for had there been a strong inner urge they would have had to give way. In earlier life the creative urge had broken through all barriers.

But this was no longer alive in the old master's spirit. His attitude was the same as Anton Bruckner's, who refused to write anything of which his 'dear God' could not approve. He knew much too well that this was the only thing that was important, and the foundation of his whole life's work.

---

[1] The widow of Adolf Paul, the writer.

ELEVEN

⟫⟫

World fame

Although the joy of creation was denied to the master in his old age, after he had retired from the world, he had practically everything else that a man could wish for. His beautiful home was full of works of art and souvenirs of a life rich in renown. He had a large library and numerous gramophone records. Through every window he could see the wide spread of the Finnish landscape that he loved so greatly. Above all, however, he had a wife who dedicated herself entirely to her 'only son' and sought to fulfil his every wish, while he was encompassed by the love and consideration of his large family. He had no more financial cares; he was prosperous and recognized throughout the world. He once said to me with pleasure, 'It is a great thing to be famous.'

Why had Sibelius withdrawn himself? Now was the time when he had so much opportunity to move about freely, to visit foreign countries and to acquaint himself with new trends in the field of culture. Why did he not show himself anywhere for decades? To all of these questions I never got a clear answer from him. Mostly he only said, 'I find it better this way,' or something else that was indefinite.

In time I understood that the explanation was not difficult to find. The great problem of his old age was a sense of guilt about the particular way of life he had chosen. It was painful for him to show himself among people, and over and over again to make conversation about his symphony that never was. The longer 'the silence of Järvenpää' lasted, the less inclination he had to forsake his entrenched position.

For any other artist it would have been almost impossible to have retreated to his home in the country for decades. But Sibelius had his rich inner life and his reputation made everything easier for him. He was not forgotten as others were, but was always having dealings with people. He heard of the triumph of his works from all over the world, and received the gratitude of thousands of admirers.

His actual rise to world fame came in the twenties, when his works were increasingly performed by many celebrated conductors. Even Arturo Toscanini, who used to be reproached for his neglect of modern music and for his restriction to the classics, was one of their number. According to a reliable source, in the years 1926–36 Toscanini conducted the Fourth Symphony on three occasions, *En Saga* five times, and *Finlandia* once—that is more often than Tchaikovsky and as much as Bach and Mozart.

The greatest enthusiasts for Sibelius among American conductors were, however, Leopold Stokowski and Serge Koussevitsky. In two years alone—1925 and 1926—Stokowski conducted works of Sibelius seventeen times in Philadelphia, his favourite being the Fifth Symphony. But he was also able to interpret the Seventh and the Fourth with great insight. When he performed the A minor Symphony in Carnegie Hall on Sibelius's seventieth birthday he asked the audience beforehand not to applaud afterwards—as though they were in church.

Serge Koussevitzky was in charge of the Boston Symphony Orchestra for almost a quarter of a century. During this time he conducted works by Sibelius on seventy-two occasions, mostly in the ten-year period from 1925 to 1935. The seven symphonies were played many, many times. In the year last mentioned the fame of the composer reached its highest peak in the United States, and all the large orchestras, and many smaller ones, played his works regularly. At the same time the general public became familiar with them through radio performances and recordings. When the audience for a series of Sunday concerts was questioned about its favourite composers a majority voted for Sibelius. The performances of his works accounted for almost 4 per cent of the total music programme: only Beethoven, Brahms, Mozart and Wagner had more performances. Five years later 450 orchestras and 5,000 music clubs celebrated his seventy-fifth birthday. In England too his reputation had been long established through numerous performances under Henry Wood and Thomas Beecham.

After 'modern music' had taken a prominent place the popularity of the Finnish composer for a time was diminished; even so his place was beyond dispute. Eugene Ormandy and other young conductors carried on the Sibelius tradition of Stokowski and Koussevitsky, and his fame spread from the United States across the whole world. In the thirties Sibelius's fan-mail came almost exclusively from the Anglo-Saxon countries, but later from all over the globe.

An outsider can scarcely imagine all that belongs to the life of one who is famous throughout the world. It is not difficult to guess that he must have had many vexations, but no one could possibly conceive of all the singular happenings that were the consequence of a great reputation. It is easy to understand the attitudes of countless old ladies—who could remember everything—who had been objects of the young Sibelius's adoration. Sibelius's reflections on this subject were: 'The older I become the more of them come to the surface; and the older they become the more deeply it appears that I was in love with them.' But who would imagine the bitter letters that he got from naïve composers who wondered how it had happened that Sibelius had become a world celebrity while they had remained completely unnoticed.

One lunatic once said that Sibelius had stolen all his works from him. Indignantly he wrote, 'Every single theme is my property and you have now achieved world fame through the labours of my mind.' Letters from the mentally ill came pretty often, for such unfortunate people often have an excess of self-confidence that draws them to famous people. In the early years I was astonished at their effusions, but Sibelius took them with lofty calm. One day when we found a second disordered letter in the letter-tray he said quietly, 'Today it seem as if we have only lunatics.' He had been considering the 'compositions'—a mass of nothing more than senseless strokes of the pen and jumbled notes—that had come with it. A pianist who had lost his balance of mind once wanted to fight a duel with the master on account of Mrs Sibelius, and named Sibelius's son-in-law as a second. Letters of this kind were on no account even acknowledged. Sibelius had once asked a psychiatrist what to do, and had been advised under all circumstances to keep quiet. But there were some people of psychopathic disposition who persecuted him on the telephone and even tried to force their way in. Sometimes it was difficult to hold them at bay.

Unfortunately one could say the same thing about perfectly normal visitors. Modesty and discretion are seldom among the qualities of those who press themselves on famous men in order to get into their circle of acquaintances. Ordinary people who were distinguished for nothing else than that they liked Sibelius's music (and sometimes not even that) thought that they were of sufficient importance to pay a visit to the much-pestered composer. Nor did they always stop at one visit. Americans especially were all the time presenting their credentials: through the Foreign Ministry, the Travel Office, a variety of other organizations, Sibelius's daughters—and even through me. Often they came without any announcement. For, so far as they were concerned, Sibelius was a kind of object on a sightseeing tour that one glanced at if one were in Finland.

Sibelius was unbelievably patient and at first rarely turned anyone away, and foreigners practically never. 'Perhaps,' he said, 'it is of some service to Finland.' Entertaining guests cost a lot of money, but Sibelius bore the expense without grumbling. He took it as a duty to act as a representative of his country, particularly on account of the large pension that he drew from the State. For a hundred-strong American choir a special cup was prepared which contained ten bottles of champagne, three of cognac, and goodness knows what else. Just at that time there was a heat wave, the like of which the guests had never experienced even in California. Afterwards they said that never in their lives had they drunk such a wonderful cup, which, in fact, Sibelius had prepared himself. Early in 1950 he told me that his annual bill for alcoholic drinks was in the region of 150,000 marks. At that time he himself hardly drank at all, but one could not offer just anything to the high-ranking guests who were then practically the only ones allowed to visit. Only the best was good enough and in Finland—a land of monopoly—good drink cost a fortune.

In later years it had been necessary to pay more attention to the selection of guests, and at the end it was only the most important who were invited. And there were enough of them too: famous conductors and performers, writers and scholars, ambassadors and diplomats, representatives of this organization or that, and well-known friends of Finland from abroad, who were under all circumstances received up to the last.

These chosen guests often gave much pleasure to Sibelius. They were the *élite* of their own profession, interesting people with whom anyone would like to talk. They moved about the world a great deal and had a lot to tell that Sibelius otherwise would never have heard. He especially enjoyed conversation with performing artists. They were always travelling and they brought reports from everywhere, including also what went on behind the scenes. He learned from them what the great conductor had said to his players when he played the Fourth Symphony, or whose ears the raging prima donna had boxed in the interval! For the most part the great artists—those who were competent to do so—talked to him as equals about artistic and human affairs. After visits of this kind Sibelius was always in good form and, laughing about them, would tell me what he had heard.

Alas! There was unfortunately a quite different category of guest: this included those mundane, boring people, who had too much money to spend on travel but too little consciousness of their own mediocrity. As a courteous host Sibelius did his best to get down to their level and to look after them. The result was always the same: the visitor left Ainola happily believing that he was a person of importance and that everything in life was marvellous. The host on the other hand sank back into his easy chair exhausted, drew a sigh of relief, and lit a cigar. Sometimes it could happen that he afterwards reproached himself for not having been polite enough to his visitor.

Journalists from all over the world, representing important newspapers and agencies, were tiresome. They said little but asked all the more and it was not easy to satisfy them. Then, to Sibelius's annoyance, they frequently wrote something quite different from what he had told them. 'They put words into my mouth that I've never said,' he complained.

The journalists obviously did their best. They were experienced and reliable men, such as important employers sent only to the famous. But they certainly had no easy job, for even those who were nearest to him found the master's flow of ideas difficult to follow, let alone a stranger who had to print what had emerged from a brief interview. It is no wonder that mistakes cropped up time after time.

From time to time Sibelius was also bothered by photographers, and in later years they too had to be rigorously sorted out. He was no grateful subject for photography; he was far too lively and, strange to relate, in front of the camera his easy, natural manner changed into stiff poses. Snapshots with flashlight were the most successful, but he disliked being photographed at all.

In August 1949 Sibelius agreed to receive Yousuf Karsh, who had gained a universal reputation through his marvellous portraits of great men, including Winston Churchill. Karsh arrived with two assistants and a van full of cameras and lighting apparatus. He set to work with true Canadian efficiency, darkened all the windows in the villa and began to take photographs. The strong light of the huge lamps quite dazzled Sibelius, which would have unsettled many photographers—but not Karsh. Quite the contrary; once more he showed what he was capable of. He made several exposures while Sibelius sat in his easy-chair with his eyes closed, and it was with one of these pictures that Karsh got just what he wanted. A more impressive photograph of Sibelius was never taken. It has something quite serene but melancholy at the same time. The master seems to be listening to inner voices— *voces intimae.*

Not infrequently journalists and photographers submitted references. They brought greetings from this or that famous conductor or virtuoso and thereby generally succeeded in being received. A journalist from Rio de Janeiro had a letter of recommendation from the leader of the Brazilian Symphony Orchestra, but apart from that he had something quite out-of-the-way to offer—for he had taken photographs of a flying saucer and now wanted to show them to Sibelius. When he visited me in Helsinki to ask permission I saw the negatives. There were five, all taken with a Rolleiflex, and there was something quite clearly to be seen on them which could have been a flying saucer. Unfortunately he didn't need the pictures since Sibelius did not invite him. I have forgotten why, but perhaps he was not well. To the Brazilian conductor in question however, he wrote a friendly letter.

Journalists and photographers went about their business even when they were a nuisance. The majority of visitors, however, had purely personal wishes. The letter-tray not infrequently contained quite straightforward begging letters, particularly after the important anniversary celebrations which were always reported in the world press. A great pile arrived after Sibelius had received the Wihuri Prize. Very often such requests touched the master's kind heart. He would murmur something about the 'poor people', stick a substantial bank-note in an envelope, and give it to me to forward on. It could be that the affecting story was made up from start to finish.

Foreign conductors and other artists not infrequently turned to Sibelius in the hope of thus being able to appear in Finland. Requests of this kind were always rejected on the ground that the master had nothing to do with the engagement of artists. It would indeed have been a bad thing if he had had anything to do in that respect, for no artist and no concert agent could have refrained from making use of advertisement of this nature, and the consequences would have been unthinkable.

Finnish artists who went abroad also solicited testimonials, for the name of their great compatriot would have been a great help. But it was only very seldom that Sibelius found himself so placed as to fulfil a request. On account of his position he had to remain unpartisan, and in other respects indeed he had carefully to consider his words and deeds. To come to a decision was sometimes much more difficult than the person in question could ever have imagined, for those who solicited his help were often friends whom Sibelius would have liked to assist. An application of this kind could worry him for a long time until he finally made up his mind. And even afterwards he tended to worry. 'I have thought about your business for days and nights,' he wrote to one friend who didn't get the testimonial he requested.

Performers who wanted to give a first performance of something by Sibelius were a group by themselves. They were for the most part Americans by whose naïveté one was sometimes astonished. An unknown lady pianist asking about a piano concerto from Sibelius also said that she would like to play unpublished works by Schumann, Liszt and Chopin, in the event of Sibelius having any. At the same time she sent him four foul and badly packed cigars which arrived in pieces. A second lady, also American, wrote that she had read in the newspaper that Sibelius was a composer, for which reason she would like to play a new piece by him.

A lot of people would have liked to possess original manuscripts of Sibelius's works, which even in his lifetime were very valuable. At the beginning of the 1950s a piano arrangement of *Valse triste* was sold in the United States for 1,500 dollars. In spite of this there were some who were so thoughtless—or impudent—as to beg for manuscripts free of charge. Other people wanted to pay, including a number of museums, which arranged funds expressly for this purpose. All the most important manuscripts, however, had for a long time been in the possession of museums and collections of MSS. in different countries. Sibelius himself had a few which were acquired by his heirs after his death.

Nevertheless those who collected manuscripts were very few in comparison with the fans who only wanted autographs. Every post brought at least half a dozen begging letters, often considerably more, particularly after the master's birthdays. They came from all over the world but were none the less standardized. The writer would say how much he liked Sibelius's music, and he would list the records he had bought for himself. It was amazing how many letters began with the simple remark: 'You are surely surprised that a total stranger writes to you . . .' But one could encounter well-thought-out and witty turns of phrase—the master was worn down with the most varied arguments and persuasions. Quite often women enlisted the aid of their children. It was not at all unusual for a letter to begin: 'I am six years old and love your music more than anything.' There followed a page or two of childish chatter (all quite clearly written by a grown-up), and right at the end came the request. A young man once began provocatively, 'I said to myself that there are two men from whom I will never get an autograph! Sibelius and Stalin.' His letter ran to three or four pages and was by no means badly written, and he got the autograph he wanted.

Finlandia and *Valse triste* were so often mentioned in these letters that in time we used them as a kind of measure. If these works and no others were mentioned we took it that the correspondent was not a serious music-lover, but had heard the pieces only in some restaurant. One evening Sibelius was in doubtful mood and suddenly said, 'We shouldn't actually talk like that. They're both good works.' That was an understandable reaction, even though he knew quite well that *Finlandia* was not one of his most significant works. As early as 1911 he had been surprised at the popularity of this 'pretty insignificant piece in relation to the rest'.

For years Sibelius sent anyone who asked an autograph, and himself paid the postage (very few gave any thought to this). Later on we had to go into the requests and select only the most important. This was especially the case in the last years when Sibelius's hand was so shaky. But it didn't please him that he couldn't fulfil every request. 'Toscanini and Strauss send everybody autographs,' he said regretfully.

Autographs too had some commercial value during Sibelius's lifetime. From some letters we received we could tell that the writer was professionally engaged in the sale of autographs. After some time the same man would turn up again in the letter-tray although he had already once got what he had asked for. In both letters he would write in sentimental terms of his great love for the master's music. People like this decorated their letters with high-falutin' titles and addresses, and on occasion one started, 'Your Excellency!' An American once put on the envelope, 'Jean Sibelius, Europe,' and nothing more. The letter arrived without any delay.

But there were people in a bigger way of business than autograph-collectors who wanted to make use of the composer's reputation. Publishers wished to have new works, while American agents came up with the most varied projects. On a number of occasions Sibelius was asked to conduct his music in the United States, and in June 1953, when he was already eighty-eight, an agency wanted to arrange a comprehensive series of concerts. Sibelius would have had to do no more than appear on the platform after each concert, for which the agency were prepared to pay him $10,000. The appearance of the Finnish master in America would have been a sensation, and the agent well knew that he would have made a small fortune.

Several times Sibelius had the chance of going to America on a pleasure-trip and at no cost to himself. He was even once offered a luxury villa, also at no charge to him, for a prolonged visit. Such offers were accompanied by attractive coloured pictures and exact descriptions of the paradisal surroundings. In America there are a lot of multi-millionaires who like to have good music and to support artists. But this is not always done merely from a love of their fellow men, for among the powerful there is an eternal battle for position and social respect, to achieve which the most diverse means are employed. A visit from a famous European composer would have had all the millionaires in the host's neighbourhood green with envy.

The name of Jean Sibelius also conferred respectability on a large number of organizations which made him an honorary member or an honorary member of its council. Every year there were more of these. First of all there was a polite inquiry as to whether membership would be agreeable. Sibelius always gave his consent in a friendly manner. It didn't need to be a zoological society of several hundred years' standing in Britain; he even wrote to a small musical society in Japan that he appreciated his election to it as an honour.

Dictators too have always patronized celebrated artists in order to gain favour for themselves. Sibelius received a high decoration from Mussolini and the Goethe Medal from Hitler, even though their ideologies were alien to him. He possessed signed letters from both. At the beginning of 1942, when the Third Reich was at its most powerful, Dr Goebbels founded a Sibelius Society. A radio commentator in Moscow spoke ironically of this and concluded by saying: 'What would the composer himself say, if he were alive?' Sibelius was sitting by the radio, laughing like anything.

With one small exception, Sibelius made no use at all of the numerous honours he received from different countries, since he never appeared anywhere. He was a 'Grand Officer' of the French Legion of Honour and the red band of this high order had once been of some help to him in Paris. He once had urgent business with a certain high authority, but because of a great press of people could not get near him. After he had stood for some time in vain in a queue he put on his red sash, and, lo and behold! all doors were immediately opened for him. Hardly had the door-keeper set his eyes on Sibelius than he bowed low and led him round the noisy throng straight to the official in question.

On the composer's days of special celebration, especially on his birthdays, a flood of congratulatory messages arrived in the master's home. Letters and telegrams came by the hundred. Festival concerts with the leading orchestras and soloists were arranged in all countries. Sibelius very often received a greeting after a concert of this kind, signed by the whole orchestra and sometimes also from prominent people who had attended. Messages also appeared with several sheets of notepaper containing the signatures of hundreds of unknown fans.

The leading conductors in the world always sent birthday greetings to Sibelius, whether they had conducted commemorative concerts or not. Great names such as those of Toscanini, Stokowski, Koussevitzky, Beecham, Cameron, Sargent, Boult, Mitropoulos, Schmidt-Isserstedt, Barbirolli, Rosbaud, Ormandy, as well as many others, were rarely missing from those who sent good wishes. The same went for the famous violinists who played the Violin Concerto all over the world. It was very seldom that these greetings came from their homes, for these virtuosi were always in transit, and they wrote from hotels or during the interval of a concert. Marian Anderson, the great Negro singer, was one of Sibelius's most loyal friends and never forgot his birthday.

Among composers the Swedes and Russians were always the most consistent in remembering Sibelius. I can't recollect ever having seen greetings from Strauss or Stravinsky. Hindemith, however, after having visited Sibelius at Ainola, sent a message for his ninetieth birthday.

Composers' associations in different countries, as also famous orchestras, broadcasting corporations and musical and many cultural bodies, were among those who sent congratulatory messages. Corporations of the Finnish cities, directors of theatres, choral societies and innumerable bodies of many different kinds did the same.

Every time there was a special occasion the Finnish Government and Parliament, it goes without saying, sent greetings to the nation's greatest son. Representatives of foreign powers brought good wishes in person. Once it happened that the British and Soviet Ambassadors—each with a huge basket of flowers—arrived at Ainola at the same time. This was when the 'cold war' between the two countries was in full swing, but Their Excellencies managed the situation supremely well, in a properly diplomatic manner, and only bombarded each other with courtesies.

After the days of high festival Ainola was like a flower-garden. There were really not enough tables, and all the floors were covered with the most splendid baskets of flowers, while even in the ante-room there was a strong scent of roses, carnations, and so on. The upper floor was also festal, with Mrs Sibelius's large bedroom full of scented flowers.

An African lady, who was among Sibelius's most devoted fans, sent a floral greeting from her homeland on every occasion. It was a huge bunch of flowers and, having been brought by air, always arrived fresh. They were the most beautiful of African flowers, but a European could not but think them somewhat rigid and dry, and mostly they had no scent. Sibelius, whose sense of smell meant so much to him, always wondered at this.

So far as the many Addresses and Diplomas that were sent to Sibelius at those times were concerned, we heaped them up on top of the piano cover in the drawing-room. Gifts included works of art, books, delicacies of many different kinds, and, above all, good cigars, which the master described as his 'staple diet'.

Everyone knew that Churchill and Sibelius were the two most famous cigar-smokers in the world. Sibelius had never tried cigarettes. Like most boys he had learned to smoke when he was at school and he had right at the start opted for a big cigar. 'I puffed away in secret in a place on the ground where all kinds of easily combustible odds and ends were kept. It was a wonder that the whole house didn't go up in flames.'

He remained true to his first choice all his life, and even towards the end of his life he always had a Havana cigar between his index- and middle-fingers. 'A novice,' he said, 'would die from the cigars I smoke in a day.'

During the war, when tobacco was strictly rationed, Sibelius had special permission from the authorities to have his needs supplied direct from the factory. Without cigars, as he once told me, he was but in a dream.

After the war, when foreign contacts were re-established, there began for Sibelius the smoker an entirely new era, not to say period of jubilee, such as he had never before experienced. In the autumn of 1948 Stokowski sent him forty-one cigars of different brands, but all of top quality, asking which he liked best so that he could thereafter always send him his favourite kind. Sibelius puffed his way ecstatically through the marvellous Havanas and at the end of September he notified the great conductor of his decision. In his letter he said:

> Paris had the difficult choice between three beauties. But I had forty-one, each as intoxicating as the others. The competition was intense, but gave me great pleasure. I pray you, maestro, accept my best thanks for your great kindness. I am fortunate in your gift and take it as an honour to receive it from you.

Hardly had this letter been dispatched than a similar, but much greater, initiative was launched in another place in the U.S.A. An organization described as the National Art Foundation arranged a collection with the title 'Cigars for Sibelius'.

As can be imagined there was an enormous response. The gentlemen of the National Arts Foundation had meant that their organization should arrange the dispatch of the cigars, but right from the start they lost all control of the situation. Almost all contributors wanted to deal with the matter personally. A stream of cigars began to come in October and reached its high point at the turn of the year. Most sent one box of cigars, but some sent as many as four. Not infrequently very large boxes with fifty or even a hundred cigars arrived. Sometimes the boxes were themselves choice pieces and beautifully decorated. When these had been emptied Sibelius found other uses for them in Ainola.

At Christmas all the tables and cupboards in the library were packed out with cigars and further consignments had to stay in great piles in a corner. 'There are already enough here,' said Sibelius, 'to last till the end. I live well now, but not for much longer.' But he lived nine more years and got through all the cigars that came in the first flood. However, fresh supplies were always arriving, and the piles in the corner of the library never came to an end. When 1950 was on the way out and Sibelius had celebrated his eighty-fifth birthday, even larger numbers of Havanas poured in.

In the autumn of 1952 Sibelius wrote to America asking that no further collections should be arranged. Nevertheless even after that many of his admirers continued regularly to send boxes of cigars. Among these donors were a great number of famous people —statesmen, industrial magnates, multi-millionaires, artists, writers, film-stars. These are only a few, taken at random, which come to mind: Cornelius Vanderbilt, Lawrence Tibbett, Sarah Churchill, Marian Anderson, Efrem Zimbalist, Arturo Toscanini, Serge Koussevitzky, John D. Rockefeller, Fritz Kreisler, Dimitri Mitropoulos, Fabian Sewitzky, Walter Damrosch, Adlai Stevenson, Kingsley Graham, Tallulah Bankhead. Dwight Eisenhower, who was not yet President, also sent a box.

Commentaries on the master's cigars proliferated in the gossip columns and the consequence was that admirers in other countries, as well as institutions and societies, joined in. The Ministry of Agriculture in Cuba, that controlled the tobacco industry in the country, sent a huge box of 200 cigars. The box was made out of a most beautiful Cuban wood and decorated with inlaid work. The cigars themselves were of a size that a normal cigar-smoker could at most only experience in a dream. In his thank-you letter Sibelius remarked how greatly he esteemed this consideration on the part of the Ministry, and he told of his uncle, the sea-captain Jean Sibelius, who had died in Havana some ninety years before. On every subsequent birthday he received a consignment of cigars from the Ministry, and several Cuban factories made him regular presents as well.

There is no doubt that fine Havana cigars gave the old man much pleasure in his old age. He was a real connoisseur and understood how to enjoy a good cigar to the full. It awoke a mood of intensity in him, and gave wings to his fancy. I remember one afternoon when Sibelius after the midday meal had smoked a cigar of a kind expressly made for Winston Churchill. A Finnish lady pianist had obtained it in Sweden from an English industrialist in order to give it to her great fellow-countryman. Sibelius smoked reverently with closed eyes and then his sixth sense awoke. After a while he said:

> I am now drawn nearer to Winston Churchill than it would ever otherwise have been possible for me. I can picture him quite exactly. The cigar is alight, and one can inhale the smoke. Cigars of this sort I could smoke one after the other. I have the impression of a man who can allow himself everything. This cigar provides me almost with a picture of Churchill's character.

I thought that cigars might have been a great help to him in composition. Now this was no longer the case, but in his last years they nonetheless gave him pleasure. Other gifts counted for less, although the number of them was almost unbelievable: table delicacies, cakes, fruit, wine and spirits, and sweetmeats; woollen goods, silks and other textiles; books, gramophone records, transistor radios and hearing-aids (which in fact he did not need); Chinese gongs, Japanese dolls and silks; beautiful handicrafts from various countries, leaves and twigs from favourite trees, garden bulbs, pressed and dried flowers, American pictures in dazzling colours, and almost anything that could be imagined.

There once came a highly distinctive gift from India—a grain of rice with 'A happy Christmas to Professor Jean Sibelius' engraved on it, and the inscription was astonishingly clear. One could almost read it with the naked eye. The donor—an Indian scholar of languages—referred in his letter to there being a small magnifying glass, which had, however, disappeared on the way. It was probably stolen. It was perhaps that kind of precious stone that is used as a magnifying glass in the Far East.

Every year a lady in Germany sent pretty little wooden figures of orchestral musicians. First came the leader of the first violins, a cellist and a trumpeter. A fresh player—sometimes two—arrived on each birthday, and Sibelius put them on the window-ledge in the library, where they went on playing until his death. Finally the harpist arrived and in thanking the lady Sibelius said that the orchestra was now able to play any symphony. He always knew how to find pretty turns of phrase promptly, for his imagination seemed to be constantly on the alert. When I was completely done in after hours of work with him the old man was still able to think of a lively message to dictate.

Anyone who sent anything received a letter of thanks. Sibelius was very strict about this. It might be thought that an acknowledgment from a world-famous man for every little courtesy is not expected. But Sibelius had a better knowledge of people. It once happened that on that account he received a sour letter from America. I had been abroad for a long time, and for that reason the master's correspondence had suffered delay. A housewife, who had sent a home-made cake, was so disappointed as to give vent to her feelings. She was, she wrote, only an ordinary housewife, but it none the less seemed proper to say thank-you even for a very modest offering, etc. By good luck the acknowledgment of the gift had already been sent before this slightly embittered missive reached Ainola. I quickly wrote a second letter, and the aggrieved lady completely thawed. Every Christmas thereafter she sent a fresh cake, and from personal experience I can testify that they always tasted excellent.

The festive days were always very severe for Sibelius. All the restless coming and going with the preparations made him tired, and he always slept badly at these times. On his birthday he had to stand and receive congratulations the whole day long, and all attempts greatly to reduce the number of guests every time proved in vain. It was only on the ninetieth birthday that none but those nearest to him were allowed to come.

However, I believe that these days gave him a great deal of pleasure and satisfaction, for they demonstrated how much his works were treasured. In later years the Finnish embassies in various parts of the world were instructed to collect all newspaper articles about the festivals and concerts given in connection with such celebrations. They were then sent in bundles to Ainola, where they were kept. Sibelius was only able cursorily to read through the most important, but that was enough, for they all said the same thing, expressing gratitude to and praise for the great Finnish composer whose work belonged to all humanity.

It was small wonder that after such occasions the eyes of the master shone brightly. He still wandered about among his many presents, sitting down to read a few messages of greeting or reviews, and then he would get up once more to go to the window. Here, in silence, he would survey the winter landscapes, as he had done a hundred times before and also in those days in which the great masterpieces had been born. These were the happiest hours of his last years, though shadowed by the approach of death.

TWELVE

▷▷▷

The final cadence

In the winter of 1948 a letter came from Edinburgh in which the Lord Provost invited Sibelius to take part in the Festival in that city in the following summer. The composer told me to write a courteous refusal. 'My doctor,' he dictated, 'has forbidden me to travel on account of my age.'

Mrs Sibelius, who was sitting near by, looked up in surprise and said, 'That is the first time I have heard you say that you are old.'

What Sibelius had said also made an impression on me. Up till now I had not been permitted to mention his age in writing letters, although it would have been the most natural reason for his many refusals. On this occasion there was no modification of the statement on reflection, although even years afterwards Sibelius did not welcome mention being made of his age.

It was clear, however, that what he had said this time was not accidental. A few months later—in May—when the whole of nature was springing to life, Sibelius pensively said to me one day:

> For the first time I have lately become aware of the fact that the period of our earthly existence is limited. During the whole of my life this idea has never actually come into my mind. It occurred to me very distinctly when I was looking at an old tree there in the garden. When we came it was very small, and I looked at it from above. Now it waves high above my head and seems to say, 'You will soon depart, but I shall stay here for hundreds more years.'

In that year, then, the powerful life force began to dry up. The fact of the passage of time was never seriously impressed on his consciousness, although there were new things and change all around him. He used only to joke about that:

> Everything around me is so very old. I have had the same tailor for sixty years. Our maid is not exactly a young girl any more. The kitchen-maid is fifty, and soon she will no longer be able to bicycle to Järvenpää twice daily. We can't expect much of the cook, I could just as well instruct the Provost's wife to do something for me.

He joked about his own age seldom, however; when he spoke about it his words had a bitter undercurrent:

> I will not speak of the fact that I am old. I find it horrible. It is very painful to be eighty. The public love artists who fall by the wayside in this life. A true artist must be down and out or die of hunger. In youth he should at least die of consumption.

The complex concerning the Eighth Symphony had so taken hold of him that he did not want to know anything about being old. It irritated him when anyone pointed out that he wasn't any longer able to do this or that. 'I don't at all understand why I should be segregated in this way,' he said. One could not give him too much help or advice. 'Why do you talk as though I were ninety years old?' he once asked his wife in injured tones. At that time he was eighty.

Newspaper reviews and articles which made mention of his age also annoyed him. A journalist on behalf of a Freemasons' periodical once came to Ainola and then wrote an account of his visit, in which he represented the composer as a tired old man: 'He says he always has music in his head but can no longer commit it to paper.' Sibelius was deeply offended and at once sent a telegram to the man. In his irritation he dictated to me as follows: 'Please make it known through your paper that I am in the best of form and am in no way deficient—Jean Sibelius.'

The journal appeared infrequently, and I had no chance to find out if this roar of the angry old lion was published or not. The lion always believed in his own power. Again and again I noted that his reaction against ageing was in no way simulated. In spirit he was always young and with an appetite for life. There was no doubt but that he spoke the truth when he said to me that it was not possible for him 'to live with his memories', as old people usually do. 'To cease to live in this way is entirely alien to me,' he asserted. 'I haven't in any way given up.'

One evening soon after his ninetieth birthday he said that in spite of his numerous descendants he couldn't imagine himself as a venerable patriarch. Then, proudly and with a very tremulous voice he said, 'Mon fils!', extending his arm and laying his hand as it were on the head of his invisible descendant. That he so quickly chose to think of himself as a French patriarch to demonstrate his meaning belonged to one of those amusing associations of ideas that to my pleasure I got to hear so frequently.

A few days later he told me good-humouredly about the famous singer, Manuel Garcia, who in 1905 had celebrated his hundredth birthday. In comparison with a centenarian even a man of ninety is relatively young, and Sibelius enjoyed chattering on about the indestructible Garcia. With due regard for the great age of the subject of the celebrations only light wines and dishes with practically no seasoning were served; but Garcia had a huge appetite and he insisted on having brandy. In the end he died as the result of a street accident.

But Sibelius was not destined to live to the age of a hundred. His powers now began slowly to ebb away. In the last few years he was no longer the 'old man' he had been. He spent much of his time sitting in the easy chair in a corner of the library. In the winter he practically never went out of doors, and in summer only when the weather was good. In August 1952 he visited Helsinki, at which time he made a long tour. He wanted to see how the city had developed—'for the last time in this life'.

Outwardly he had become much quieter. The briskness and vivacity so typical of him had by now forsaken him. He received guests very seldom and in general his interest for what was going on in the world at large seemed to have departed. Only his attachment to nature was as it had previously been. One could appreciate that when he used to walk in the Ainola woods when it was warm, or when in winter he used to stand at the window and in silence contemplate the broad expanse of snow-covered fields. 'It is difficult,' he would say, 'to leave life when nature is so very beautiful.'

He said nothing about composing any more. He had finally given up; the tragedy of the Eighth Symphony troubled him no longer. At least he gave no outward sign that it did.

But he found no peace of mind, for it had ever been a trait of his character to worry overmuch over trivial things. This characteristic was clearly a consequence of his powerful imagination. He complained about entirely unimportant matters, which took on unreasonable dimensions in his mind. At night he was tormented by thinking about his youthful works as well as all kinds of other affairs of much less consequence. The same tiny detail could nag at him for weeks. When finally he forgot it, there was another to take its place, and this went on growing in his imagination. It pained me greatly to see him suffer for no reason at all.

It is not unusual for old men to complain about trivial things. Often the real cause of evil is hidden deep in the mind. The approach of death, which even if never mentioned is never forgotten, causes irritation and a melancholy attitude which expresses itself in this manner.

I would like to think that this was not the case with Sibelius. I believe rather that the number of small things about which he worried kept him from thinking of his approaching end. Before 1948 he never spoke of it, and later he avoided the subject in the presence of his wife. But the two of us talked several times about the world to come, and I never noticed that the subject disturbed him. He said: 'That is something one must take quite naturally. We all die once.'

It would indeed happen that he made jokes over his final departure. He would be a great sinner: 'It will cause an unparalleled sensation when I enter heaven. Everyone will look around and ask, "What is he doing here?" But I can lay before St Peter plenty of certificates and supporting evidence.'

He once commented that in his life he had done nothing but evil: 'According to Buddha one should think only on one's good deeds when one dies. But what shall I think on?' As he said this he laughed gaily.

An American musician once asked to visit him during the next summer, adding the phrase, 'before I die'. Sibelius read the letter through and quietly remarked: 'It is unlikely that we shall meet one another. In the summer I shall hardly still be alive. And so far as a later meeting is concerned it is not certain that we shall go to the same place.'

That made him remember a comic episode from his time in Berlin. One evening he was working in his room when a great storm broke over the city. The maid, who was a Mohammedan, was frightened, and rushed to him to ask if she could sit by his work-table. 'Of course, you can stay here if you are afraid,' said Sibelius, 'but it is much better that you sit some distance away from me—say, over there by the door. Otherwise it could happen that if the lightning should strike us both you would go with me into the wrong heaven.'

Sibelius believed in a life after death, as I was more than once able to establish. 'I shall indeed soon see it,' he said in the summer of 1957 when we had once more been discussing the matter of the hereafter. One of the last notes I made confirmed that he held this belief. We were talking about one of the friends of his youth, who had long since died. Sibelius told me something about him and suddenly and quite spontaneously said, 'I wonder if he sees us and hears what we are saying?'

During his last months the master's home seemed strangely altered. At no previous time had I had the feeling that one lived there no longer in the present but in a distant past. The life force of the owner no more irradiated the place. He was in retreat from life, and he knew well that his last hour would soon strike. How could he, who had the gift of spiritual vision, not have had some awareness of it?

In the summer of 1957 he seldom went out. His interest in the affairs of this world, that had always been so lively, more and more left him. I sometimes got the impression that he compelled himself to focus his attention on the prevailing issues of the time in order to participate in life. 'Every day in my old age is more important than I can say,' he said to me shortly before his death. 'It will never return. When one takes one's leave of life one notices how much one has left undone.'

From the gist of our previous conversation I understood at that time that he did not refer to his work as a composer. He was thinking of the people with whom he had lived, of his loved ones, who had so much to thank him for, but to whom he would have given even more. For the greatest thing about him, his love of humanity, never lost its power. Even in the hour of death his look was as warming as the light of the sun.

★   ★   ★

On Wednesday 18th September several large formations of cranes flew over the master's home on their long journey south. Sibelius hurried to the veranda and to his joy saw that the birds were flying low. They were also very audible. Then, suddenly, one crane detached itself from the rest, slowly circled over Ainola and then rejoined its fellow-travellers. Soon they all vanished into the blue horizon.

This was the farewell of the migrating birds.

On that day and also on the next nobody noticed anything exceptional about Sibelius. He spent his time as usual, and on Thursday he spoke on the telephone to Sir Malcolm Sargent, who was then conducting in Helsinki.

On Friday morning immediately after waking up he complained of giddiness. As usual, however, he read the newspaper in bed and then dressed himself. At one o'clock as he was sitting at luncheon he collapsed. The doctor, who was called immediately, diagnosed a haemorrhage of the brain. Sibelius was still fully conscious but certain symptoms of a stroke were evident. He didn't say much and his words were blurred, but he had no pain and when Mrs Sibelius asked he answered quite intelligibly that he was all right.

At four o'clock in the afternoon he lost consciousness, but the flame of life flickered for several hours more. It was at a quarter to nine that the soul left the body.

What marked the passing of the great composer was as might have been expected and, one might say, almost predetermined. No man could have wished for a more beautiful death. He crossed the frontier peacefully and without effort; it was not much different from his going out of his house, as he had gone hundreds of times, with the sun shining in a blue sky. He died, as he had been born, on a Friday. At the time of his death Malcolm Sargent was conducting the Fifth Symphony, the work that symbolized the peak of his fame, in Helsinki.

Next morning the newspapers reported the death of the master with huge pictures and headlines spread across eight columns. At midday the President of Finland spoke an appreciation on the radio and of the significance for the Finnish people of the works of the great man so recently deceased. 'After hundreds of years, generations yet to come will draw strength from his massive achievement.' To some extent what Sir Leslie Munro, Chairman of the General Assembly of the United Nations, said in his memorial speech was a continuation of these words. 'Sibelius belongs to the whole world. Through his music he has enriched the whole of humanity.'

The news spread through the world press like a great wave, and newspapers in all countries commented on the death of the Finnish master. There were headings in heavy black type and long special articles. 'Sibelius kept the secret of the Eighth Symphony,' announced a caption across seven columns of the *Daily Mail*. At the same time broadcasting stations all over the world said that even without the Eighth Symphony his was a great contribution to world culture, and the air resounded with his music.

On Saturday messages of sympathy began; and letters, telegrams and flowers, poured into the silent home of the master. But not only there. The death of the great composer was an occasion for national mourning, which was understood everywhere abroad. The President, the State Council, the Ministry for Foreign Affairs, and Finnish Missions in all countries received official messages of condolence. Among them were some from heads of States, including those from the three Scandinavian kings. The American Ambassador sent a telegram in which he expressed sympathy in the name of the people of the U.S.A.

For the last time Ainola was transformed into a flower garden full of scent. Fresh messages of sympathy were continually being received by the mourning widow, whose solicitude for the master was now, after sixty-five years of life together, at an end. She bore her sorrow with dignity, as she had borne all others in her life. She knew that she need not be completely severed from her loved one.

The last resting-place of the composer was a small, sunny plot in the garden to the south of the villa. The site of the grave had been long arranged. The cemetery in Järvenpää had been thought of too, but Sibelius himself made the decision: 'They will put up a larger monument to me than that of Aleksis Kivi.[1] And that I would not like.'

On the last Sunday and Monday of September the Finnish people took leave of its greatest son. In a dim autumnal light the funeral carriage with the black coffin covered with laurel wreaths drove the four miles from Ainola to the cathedra in Helsinki. At first there followed only the few cars with the nearest relatives. But once on the main road other cars joined the funeral procession, which finally stretched for several kilometres.

Brilliant flames from burning tar lit the square before the cathedral as the funeral carriage stopped in front of its broad steps. To the music of a Bach Adagio twelve orchestra players carried the coffin to the altar, where seven tall candles with white lilies around them symbolized the master's seven symphonies. Four students of the Conservatory of Music, which now bore the name of the great Finnish master, were the first representatives of the general student body to undertake the duties of a guard of honour, in which in the course of the night all the high schools and student associations took part. At nine o'clock at night the doors were opened for the crowd patiently waiting in front of the church. In those hours 17,000 men and women silently passed by the coffin.

Next morning before the funeral service wreaths were laid. It was very still in the church as different delegations—more than a hundred in all—one after the other paid their last tributes. The wreaths of the State Council and of Parliament were the last to be brought. When the church clock began to strike twelve the black coffin was almost completely covered with thousands of sweet-smelling flowers.

After the service only two people were permitted to lay wreaths: Aino Sibelius and the President of the Republic. Bowed deep but composed, the master's widow sat before the coffin. She had not thought that she would have to experience this hard day. In the

[1] Aleksis Kivi (1834–72), Finnish national poet.

last years there was sometimes a small contention concerning which of the two would die first. 'He is under the delusion that I will be a widow,' Aino Sibelius once said to me, and laughed. But Providence had willed that it should not be a delusion. To the end Sibelius kept with him her of whom he had said that without her he would not have been able to accomplish his life's work. Surely more than anyone else she was moved by the *Il tempo largo* of the Fourth Symphony, which was played during the funeral service in the cathedral as Sibelius had wished.

For the last time that day Aino Sibelius was able to see for herself what great love and admiration the Finnish people had for him to whom she had devoted her life. People stood in their thousands in the streets as the funeral carriage left the capital, with all its flags at half-mast, and drove slowly through the guard of honour of the student associations back to Ainola to the last resting-place of the master.

EPILOGUE

▷▷▷▷▷▷▷▷▷▷▷▷▷▷▷▷▷▷▷▷ ▷▷▷▷▷▷▷▷▷▷▷▷▷▷▷▷▷▷▷▷▷▷▷▷▷▷▷

The place of Sibelius in the history of music

A young Finnish woman who was a journalist once wrote an essay which began as follows: 'Bach, Beethoven, Sibelius: three great composers—perhaps the greatest.' She showed me her manuscript and I suggested that she should omit the last three words. This she did.

When a small nation of four million people produces an artist whose acclaim is truly universal it is easy to understand that in his own country his importance is unreasonably exaggerated. This is particularly the case when admirers have only a slender idea of musical history.

It is, then, much more significant that foreign critics and scholars, important ones among them, have often compared Sibelius with Beethoven. Cecil Gray has gone so far as to say that Sibelius is the only true symphonic composer since Beethoven, and not only the greatest figure of his own generation but one of the greatest in the history of music. One finds similar enthusiastic assertions in what other English and Americans have written.

How much truth is there in this attitude?

In so far as I am entitled to one my view has always been that there are four great composers: Bach, Haydn, Mozart and Beethoven. Perhaps someone might add one or two composers to this list, but these four in any case up to now remain unsurpassed and in all likelihood will remain so for a very long time to come. The range of the works of these giants alone silences any comparison. In this respect one does not need to waste words over Bach, Haydn and Mozart. Beethoven wrote 'only' nine symphonies, seven concertos and ten overtures, but a considerable amount of chamber music of the highest quality, an opera, two masses, an oratorio, and a large number of other vocal works as well. In addition to his seven symphonies, symphonic poems and orchestral suites, Sibelius has written only one concerto and one string quartet that are significant.

The comparison appears somewhat different when we place Sibelius alongside the Romantics. But does he belong to them or to a later epoch in music? Over this question a great deal of ink has flowed. There are many who regard him as a pure national-romantic composer and emphasize the programme element in his music—even when it is not present. Others describe him as a modern composer, while the classical clarity of his last works on the other hand furnishes quite a new image.

No one will deny that Sibelius was very closely associated with Romanticism, even though he was born more than half a century after Schumann, Chopin and Mendelssohn, and a quarter of a century after Tchaikovsky and Dvořák. Especially in his early years he showed all the features of Romanticism: subjective experience, a prolific imagination and capacity for powerful projection of the emotions. Most of the Romantics were torn apart inwardly, and unbalanced, while many were mentally sick. Even Sibelius experienced mental unrest and disequilibrium. Mental illness occurred among his nearest relatives, and his own eccentricity must sometimes have aroused concern.

But there was one essential difference between Sibelius and his forerunners. In the case of most Romantics it is notable that their creative work showed no development, but to some extent dropped from heaven already prepared. Mendelssohn was able to write as well at the age of seventeen, when he wrote the *Midsummer Night's Dream* overture, as shortly before his death. Similarly with Schumann's *Papillons* and Chopin's 'Là ci darem' Variations. None of the Romantic composers lived long, with the exception of

Brahms, but although he lived to the age of sixty-four his style remained fundamentally unaltered.

It was quite otherwise with Sibelius. He began by being a strongly emotional nationalist-Romantic, who transferred himself to the province of absolute music in his symphonies. Increasingly he alienated himself from Romanticism, to create in several works of importance a quite original and modern style, and finally to reach a conclusion in classical clarity.

An American professor of music in a biography of Sibelius that is as superficial as it is negative has said that the composer had let himself be guided by purely external factors. He had become sensitive to critics, conditioned himself after what they said, and had taken external factors in general into consideration in regard to his works.

I can only describe this interpretation as astonishing. I am of a quite contrary opinion, that to a greater extent than many other composers of distinction Sibelius was dependent on his own inner life. While Mendelssohn and Chopin, for example (not to speak of Haydn and Mozart), in spite of all individuality, held themselves free in relation to the creative process, and to a certain degree stood 'outside' it, the music of Sibelius was bound fast to his inner experiences. He began his career at a time when the Finns were fighting for their freedom, and was deeply interfused with the mood of the country. Thus came the *Kalevala* works and a series of works of national character. In the first two symphonies, however, this is to be detected not as a programme but as a state of mind. With advancing age deeper matters began to concern the composer, which found expression in absolute music. The period in which he was always under threat of sickness, accompanied by other severe inner experiences, produced works of corresponding character. The Fourth Symphony, *Voces intimae*, the tone-poem *Luonnotar* and other works appeared, all of which reflect the intensity of this time. In his last works, on the other hand, the state of transfiguration and peace of mind of the old man was clad in classical forms.

In this sense I have understood the development of Sibelius the composer. It went hand in hand with his development as a person.

He was the most subjective, the most personal of all Romantics. He lived his music.

There is a further piece of evidence. However different his works from different periods can be they all have the unmistakable Sibelius quality. Most often this is taken to be something very Finnish, not only by Sibelius's fellow-countrymen but also by foreigners. What is this Sibelius-Finnish quality in his music? I believe I scarcely err when I say that this general quality was the expression of a strong spiritual experience, and that this lasted throughout life. The connection with the natural beauty of his country was rooted deep in Sibelius's feelings and became almost like a religion. It sounded out in all the music that he wrote.

This firm connection of the inner life with his creativity cannot have been without influence on the difficulties experienced in his work. It was expressed, perhaps, in the words which Sibelius himself used: 'Those composers are the least fortunate for whom work is an inner compulsion. I am just such an unfortunate composer.'

In the 1930s, and even later, Sibelius more often than not was described as a conspicuously modern composer. That at one time he was is not to be doubted. Compared with him Tchaikovsky and Dvořák were conservative and traditional. But even in so far as he was modern Sibelius was extremely personal, as is testified especially by his Fourth Symphony. He never, however, followed certain tendencies, which was perhaps the reason for younger musicians denying his modernity.

The remaining question is whether Sibelius exercised an influence on the development of music. There are those among musicologists who hold that he created new symphonic forms. Whether that is so or not lies outside my competence since, by profession, I am no music theorist. The influence of Sibelius may indeed clearly be discerned in the works of some composers, not all of whom are Finnish. But he never collected a group of disciples around him and nothing like a school—as for example in the case of Schoenberg—ever emerged. He was much too personal, much too individual and exclusive, for that. In the history of music he was an independent figure, a lone wolf, who trod his own paths in the broad woodlands.

No one should take it that through this statement I wish to reduce the importance of the Finnish master as a creative spirit. Everything that I have written here has been done in full recognition of and admiration for his work. In the history of music there is a handful of great composers—some thirty or forty. Jean Sibelius is among them and will always have a place of his own.

LIST OF WORKS

▷▷▷

Abbreviations

A	Affärstryckeriet, Turku		Accepted Masons of the State of New York
AH	Abraham Hirsch, Stockholm	MA	Musices Amantes, Turku
AL	Axel Lindgren, Helsinki	MM	Muntra Musikanter, Helsinki
BH	Breitkopf & Härtel, Wiesbaden	MK	Musiikkikeskus, Helsinki
C	Chappell & Co., London	NMF	Nordiska Musikförlaget, Stockholm
D	Delanchy-Dupré, Asnières (Seine)	SÄV	Sävelistö
F	Fazerin Musiikkikauppa, Helsinki	SB	Silver Burdett, Boston
		SFV	Svenska Folkskolans Vänner, Helsinki
FW	Fazer & Westerlund, Helsinki	SL	Suomen Laulajain ja Soittajain Liitto, Helsinki
H	Wilhelm Hansen Musikforlag, Copenhagen	SM	Suomen Musiikkilehti, Helsinki
JW	J. Wikstedtin Kivipaino, Helsinki	T	F. Tilgmann, Helsinki
KO	Kustannusosakeyhtiö Otava, Helsinki	UE	Universal-Edition, Vienna
KW	K. F. Wasenius, Helsinki	W	R. E. Westerlund OY, Helsinki
L	Robert Lienau, Berlin-Lichterfelde	WS	Werner Söderström Osakeyhtiö, Helsinki
LM	Laulu-Miehet, Helsinki	YL	Ylioppilaskunnan Laulajat, Helsinki
M	Grand Lodge of Free and		

The date indicates the year of composition. Each entry for an orchestral work includes details of the instrumentation, to be read according to the following example: 2222/4331/12/1/str. = 2 flutes, 2 oboes, 2 clarinets, 2 bassoons / 4 horns, 3 trumpets, 3 trombones, 1 tuba / timpani, 2 percussive instruments / harp / strings.

Works for Orchestra

Opus

6. *Cassazione*, 1904, MS.
   1. 2222/4231/10/0/str. 2. 2020/2110/10/0/str.
9. *En Saga*, tone-poem, 1892, rev. 1901, BH. 2222/4331/01/0/str.
10. *Karelia*, Overture, 1893, BH. 3222/4331/11/0/str.
11. *Karelia* Suite. 1893, BH.
    1. Intermezzo. 2. Ballade. 3. Alla marcia. 3222/4331/11/0/str.
14. *Rakastava* (The lover), 1911, BH. (Rewritten. See Choral Works).
    1. The Lover. 2. The Path of the Beloved. 3. Good-Night-Farewell. 0000/0000/11/0/str.
16. *Vårsång* (Spring song), Impromptu, 1894, BH. 2222/4331/11/0/str.
22. *Lemminkäinen*, four legends, BH.
    1. Lemminkäinen and the Maidens of the Island, 1895, rev. 1897, 1939. 2222/4330/12/0/str. 2. The Swan of Tuonela, 1893, rev. 1897, 1900. 0112/4030/11/1/str. 3. Lemminkäinen in Tuonela, 1895, rev. 1897, 1939. 2222/4330/03/0/str. 4. Lemminkäinen's Home-coming, 1895, rev. 1897, 1900. 2222/4331/13/0/str.
25. *Scènes historiques I*, 1899, rev. 1911, BH.
    1. All' Overtura. 2222/4330/10/0/str. 2. Scena. 3. Festivo. 2222/4330/13/0/str.
26. *Finlandia*, tone-poem, 1899, BH. 2222/4331/12/0/str.
39. Symphony No. 1 in E minor, 1899, BH.
    1. *Andante ma non troppo—Allegro energico*. 2. *Andante (man on troppo lento)*. 3. *Scherzo (Allegro)*. 4. *Finale (Quasi una fantasia)*· 2222/4331/12/1/str.
42. Romance in C major for string orchestra, 1903, BH. Also known as *Andante for strings*.
43. Symphony No. 2 in D major, 1901–2, BH.
    1. *Allegro—Poco allegro*. 2. *Tempo andante ma rubato—Allegro—Andante sostenuto*. 3. *Vivacissimo*. 4. *Allegro moderato*. 2222/4331/10/0/str.
45. 1. *The Dryad*, tone-poem, 1910, BH. 3232/4331/02/0/str.
    2. *Dance Intermezzo*, 1907, BH. 2121/4200/11/1/str. 1020/2100/11/0/str.
49. *Pohjola's Daughter*, tone-poem, 1906, L. 3333/4431/10/1/str.
52. Symphony No. 3 in C major, 1907, L.
    1. *Allegro moderato*. 2. *Andantino con moto, quasi allegretto*. 3. *Moderato*. 2222/4230/10/0/str.
53. *Pan and Echo*, dance intermezzo, 1906, L. 3333/4431/10/1/str.

55. *Night-ride and Sunrise*, tone-poem, 1907, L. 3233/4231/13/0/str.
59. *In Memoriam*, funeral march, 1909, BH. 2333/4331/13/0/str.
63. Symphony No. 4 in A minor, 1911, BH.
    1. *Tempo molto moderato, quasi adagio.* 2. *Allegro molto vivace.*
    3. *Il tempo largo.* 4. *Allegro.* 2222/4230/11/0/str.
64. *The Bard*, tone-poem, 1913, rev. 1914, BH. 2232/4230/11/1/str.
66. *Scènes historiques II*, 1912, BH.
    1. The Chase. 2222/4000/10/0/str. 2. Love Song. 2222/4000/10/1/
    str. 3. At the Drawbridge. 3222/4000/11/1/str.
73. *The Oceanides* (Aallottaret), tone-poem, 1914, rev. 1914, BH.
    3333/4330/12/2/str.
82. Symphony No. 5 in E flat major, 1915, rev. 1916, 1919, H.
    1. *Molto moderato—Allegro moderato.* 2. *Andante mosso quasi
    allegretto.* 3. *Allegro molto.* 2222/4330/10/0/str.
96. 1. *Valse lyrique*, 1920, H. 2222/4230/11/0/str. 2. *Autrefois, scène
    pastorale*, 1919, H. 2022/2000/10/0/str. 3. *Valse chevaleresque*,
    1920, H. 2222/4230/11/0/str.
98. 1. *Suite mignonne*, 1921, C. a. *Petite scène*, b. *Polka*, c. *Epilogue.*
    2000/0000/00/str.
    2. *Suite champêtre* for string orchestra, 1921, H. a. *Pièce carac-
    téristique*, b. *Mélodie élégiaque*, c. *Danse.*
100. *Suite caractéristique* for harp and string orchestra, 1922, MS.
    1. *Vivo*, 2. *Lento*, 3. *Commodo.*
104. Symphony No. 6 in D minor, 1923, AH.
    1. *Allegro molto moderato.* 2. *Allegretto quasi andante.* 3. *Poco
    vivace.* 4. *Allegro molto.* 2232/4330/10/1/str.
105. Symphony No. 7 in C major, 1924, H. In one movement. First
    name *Fantasia sinfonica.* 2222/4330/10/0/str.
112. *Tapiola*, tone-poem, 1926, BH. 3333/4330/10/0/str.

Andante festivo for string orchestra and timpani *ad lib.*, 1922, W.
Andante for strings, see p. 137, Opus 42.
Andante lirico, for string orchestra, see: *Impromptu* (below).
Ballet Scene, 1891, MS. 2222/4221/02/0/str.
Ballet Scene, 1909, MS. 2222/4230/11/0/str.
Björneborgarnes March, arr. for orchestra, 1900, MS. 2222/4330/02/
0/str.
Cortège, 1901, MS.
Impromptu, for string orchestra, 1894, MS. Probably same as
Andante lirico, see p. 142, Opus 5.
Minuetto, 1894, MS. Also known as *Minuet-Impromptu* and *Tempo
di minuetto* 1122/4331/01/0/str.
Morceau romantique sur un motif de M. Jacob de Julin, 1925, MS.
Also known as *Pièce romantique.*

Overture in E major, 1890–1, MS. 2222/4221/11/0/str.

Overture in A minor, 1902, MS. 2222/4421/10/0/str.

Presto, for string orchestra, MS. See p. 141 Opus 4, String Quartet in B flat major.

Promotiomarssi (Academic march), for orchestra, 1919, MS. 2222/4200/11/1/str.

Scherzo, for string orchestra, 1894, MS. Probably arrangement of the *Presto* movement from the String Quartet in B flat major, see p. 141, Opus 4.

Valse triste, see below, Opus 44.

For Solo Instrument and Orchestra

Opus

47. Concerto in D minor for violin and orchestra, 1903, rev. 1905, L.
    1. *Allegro moderato.* 2. *Adagio di molto.* 3. *Allegro ma non tanto.*
    2222/4230/10/0/str.

69. Two serenades for violin and orchestra, BH.
    No. 1, D major, 1912. 2222/4000/10/0/str. No. 2, G minor, 1913.
    2222/4000/11/0/str.

77. Two pieces for violin (or cello) and orchestra, 1914, H.
    1. *Cantique* (*Laetare anima mea*). 2020/2000/10/1/str. 2. *Devotion* (*Ab imo pectore*). 2012/4030/0/str.

87. Humoresques I–II for violin and orchestra, 1917, H.
    No. 1, D minor, 2222/2000/10/0/str. No. 2, D major, 0000/2000/10/0/str.

89. Humoresques III–VI for violin and orchestra, 1917, H.
    No. 3, G minor, string orchestra. No. 4, G minor, string orchestra. No. 5, E flat major, 2022/0000/00/0/str. No. 6, G minor, 2002/0000/00/0/str.

Incidental music

Opus

8. Mikael Lybeck: *Ödlan* (The lizard), 1909, MS. Act II, scenes 1 & 3, for solo violin and string quintet.

27. Adolf Paul: *King Christian II*, 1898, BH.
    1. *Elegie*, 2. *Musette*, 3. *Minuetto*, 4. *Song of the Spider*, 5. *Nocturne*, 6. *Serenade*, 7. *Ballade*. 2222/4230/11/1/str. and voice. Suite for orchestra less no. 4.

44. Arvid Järnefelt: *Kuolema* (Death), 1903, MS. Six scenes for string orchestra, bass drum and church bell.
    No. 1 revised as *Valse triste*, 1904, BH. 1010/2000/10/0/str. Nos. 3 & 4 revised as Scene with Cranes, 1906, MS.

46. Maurice Maeterlinck: *Pelléas et Mélisande*, concert suite, 1905, L.

1. At the Castle Gate (Prelude, Act I, Scene 1). 2. Mélisande (Prelude, Act I, Scene 2). 3. At the Seashore ('Melodrama', Act I, Scene 4). 4. At the Spring in the Park (Prelude, Act II, Scene 1). 5. Three Blind Sisters (Mélisande's Song, Act III, Scene 2). 6. Pastorale ('Melodrama', Act III, Scene 4). 7. Mélisande at the Spinning-wheel (Prelude, Act III, Scene 1). 8. Entr'acte (Prelude, Act IV, Scene 1). 9. Mélisande's Death (Prelude, Act V, Scene 2). 1122/2000/11/0/str. Unpublished: Prelude, Act IV, Scene 2, and Mélisande's Song, No. 5, original version.

51. Hjalmar Procopé: *Belsazars gästabud* (Belshazzar's feast). 1906. Original score; MS.
    1. Alla marcia (Act 1). 2. Nocturne (Prelude, Act II). 3. The Jewish Girl's Song (Act II). 4. Allegretto (Act III). 5. Dance of Life (Act III). 6. Dance of Death (Act III). 7. Tempo sostenuto (Act IV). 8. Allegro (Act IV). 1020/2000/03/0/str.
    Concert Suite, L.
    1. Oriental Procession (No. 1). 2. Solitude (accompaniment for No. 3). 3. Night Music (No. 2). 4. Khadra's Dance (Nos. 5 & 6). 2120/2000/03/0/str.

54. August Strindberg: *Svanevit* (Swanwhite), 1908. Original score has 14 scenes, MS. 1010/2000/11/0/str.
    Concert Suite, L.
    1. The Peacock, 2. The Harp, 3. The Maiden with the Roses, 4. Listen, the Robin Sings, 5. The Prince Alone, 6. Swanwhite and the Prince, 7. Song of Praise. 2222/4000/11/1/str.

60. W. Shakespeare: *Twelfth Night*, 1909, BH. Two songs with guitar or piano:
    1. *Kom nu hit, död!* (Act II, Scene 4). With harp and string orchestra, 1957, MS. 2. *Och när som jag var en liten smådräng* (Act V, Scene 1).

62. Arvid Järnefelt: *Kuolema* (Death), 1911, BH.
    1. Canzonetta for string orchestra. 2. Valse romantique. 2020/2000/10/0/str.

71. P. Knudsen and M. T. Bloch: *Scaramouche*, tragic pantomime, 1913, H. 2222/4100/12/1/str.

83. Hugo von Hofmannsthal: *Jedermann* (Everyman), 1916, MS. For mixed chorus, piano, organ and orchestra. 2121/2200/11/0/str.

109. W. Shakespeare: *The Tempest*, 1925, H. Original score: 34 parts for soloists, mixed chorus, harmonium and orchestra, MS. Arranged for concert performance:
    1. Prelude. 3232/4331/13/0/str. 2. Suite No. 1: a. The Oak Tree, b. Humoresque, c. Caliban's Song, d. The Harvesters, e. Canon, f. Scena, g. Intrada—Berceuse. h. Entr'acte—Ariel's Song,

i. The Storm. 3232/4331/13/1/str. 3. Suite No. II. a. Chorus of the Winds, b. Intermezzo, c. Dance of the Nymphs, d. Prospero, e. Song I, f. Song II, g. Miranda, h. The Naiads, i. Dance Episode. 2222/4000/10/1/str.

Adolf Paul: *Die Sprache der Vögel* (The language of the birds), 1911, MS. Wedding March for Act III. 2130/0220/13/0/str.

Karelia music, original score, 1893, MS. 1. *Overture* (Opus 10). 2. *Più lento*. 3. *Moderato assai*. 4. *March in the Old Style* (Opus 11, no. 1). 5. *Tempo di minuetto* (Opus 11, no. 2). 6. *Moderato ma non tanto*. 7. *Alla marcia—'Based on an old motif'* (Opus 11, no. 3). 8. *Vivace*. 9. *Moderato—Allegro molto—Vivace molto—Maestoso e largamente* (The Finnish national anthem *Vårtland* by Fredrik Pacius). 2222/4331/11/0/str.

'Press Celebrations' music, 1899. Tableau I: *All' Overtura* (see p. 137, Opus 25, no. 1). Tableau II: *Andante ma non troppo lento*, MS. 2222/4230/02/0/str. Tableau III: *Festivo* (see p. 137, Opus 25, no. 3). Tableau IV: *Scena* (see p. 137, Opus 25, no. 2). Tableau V: *Grave*, MS. 2222/4330/11/0/str. Tableau VI: *Finlandia*, see p. 137, Opus 26).

Chamber Music

Opus
2. Two Pieces for violin, with piano, 1888, rev. 1912, UE.
   1. Romance in B minor. 2. Epilogue (first title *Perpetuum mobile*).
4. String Quartet in B flat major, 1889, MS.
20. *Malinconia* for cello, with piano, 1901, BH.
56. String quartet in D minor (*Voces intimae*), 1909, L.
    1. *Andante—Allegro molto moderato*. 2. *Vivace*. 3. *Adagio di molto*. 4. *Allegretto (ma pesante)*. 5. *Allegro*.
78. Four Pieces for violin (or cello), with piano, H.
    1. Impromptu, 1915. 2. Romance, 1915. 3. Religioso, 1919. 4. Rigaudon, 1915.
79. Six Pieces for violin, with piano, 1915, H.
    1. Souvenir. 2. Tempo di minuetto. 3. Danse caractéristique. 4. Sérénade. 5. Dance idyll. 6. Berceuse.
80. Sonatina in E major for violin and piano, 1915, H.
    1. *Lento—Allegro*. 2. *Andantino*. 3. *Lento—Allegretto—Vivace*.
81. Five Pieces for violin, with piano, 1915, W.
    1. Mazurka. 2. Rondino. 3. Waltz. 4. Aubade. 5. Minuetto.
102. *Novelette* for violin and piano, 1923, H.
106. Five *Danses champêtres* for violin and piano, 1925, H.
115. Four Pieces for violin, with piano, 1929, BH.
    1. On the Heath. 2. Ballade. 3. Humoresque. 4. The Bells.

116. Three Pieces for violin, with piano, 1929, BH.
    1. Scène de danse. 2. Danse caractéristique. 3. Rondeau romantique.

Andante cantabile for violin and piano, 1887, MS.
Andante festivo for string quartet, 1922, W.
Andantino, for clarinet, 2 cornets, 2 horns, baritone and tuba, 1890–1, MS.
Andantino for cello and piano, 1884, MS.
Fantasia for cello and piano, 1884, MS.
Minuetto, for clarinet, 2 cornets, 2 horns, baritone and tuba, 1890, MS.
Quartet for piano and strings in E minor, 1881–2, MS.
Quartet for piano, two violins and cello in C major, 1891, MS.
Quartet for piano, harmonium, violin and cello in G minor, 1887, MS.
Quintet for piano and strings in G minor, 1889, MS.
Rondo for viola and piano, 1893, MS.
Sonata for violin and piano in D minor, 1881–3, MS.
Sonata for violin and piano in F major, 1886(?), MS.
String quartet in E flat major, 1885, MS.
String quartet in A minor, 1889, MS.
Suite for string trio in A major, 1889, MS.
Theme and Variations for string quartet, in C sharp minor, 1888, MS.
Trio in A minor, for violin, cello and piano, 1881–2, fragments, MS.
Trio in G minor, for violin, viola and piano, 1885 (?), MS.
Trio for violin, cello and piano (so-called Korpo Trio), 1887.
Trio in C major, for violin, cello and piano (so-called Loviisa-Trio), 1888, MS.
Vattendroppar (Water drops), for violin and cello pizzicato, 1876, MS.

Piano Works

Opus
5. Six Impromptus, 1893, BH. Nos. 5 & 6 arranged for string orchestra under the title of *Impromptu*.
12. Sonata in F major, 1893, BH.
    1. *Allegro molto*. 2. *Andantino*. 3. *Vivacissimo*.
24. Ten Pieces, BH.
    1. Impromptu, 1894. 2. Romance in A major, 1894. 3. Caprice, 1895. 4. Romance in D minor, 1895. 5. Waltz in E major, 1895. 6. Idyll, 1898. 7. Andantino, 1898. 8. Nocturne, 1900. 9. Romance in D flat major, 1903. 10. Barcarola, 1903.
34. Ten small pieces, 1914–16, BH, Nos. 7–10 W.
    1. Waltz. 2. Dance Air. 3. Mazurka. 4. Humorous. 5. Drollery.

6. Rêverie. 7. Pastoral Dance. 8. The Harper. 9. Reconnaissance. 10. Souvenir.

40. *Pensées lyriques*, 1912–1914, BH, Nos. 9 & 10 W.
    1. Valsette. 2. Chant sans paroles. 3. Humoresque. 4. Minuetto. 5. Berceuse. 6. Pensée mélodique. 7. Rondoletto. 8. Scherzando. 9. Petite Sérénade. 10. Polonaise.

41. *Kyllikki*, three lyric pieces, 1904, BH.
    1. Largamente—Allegro. 2. Andantino. 3. Commodo.

58. Ten Pieces, 1909, BH.
    1. Rêverie. 2. Scherzino. 3. Air varié. 4. The Shepherd. 5. The Evening. 6. Dialogue. 7. Tempo di minuetto. 8. Fisher Song. 9. Sérénade. 10. Summer Song.

67. Three Sonatinas, 1912, BH.
    No. 1 in F sharp minor, a. Allegro, b. Largo, c. Allegro. No. 2 in E major, a. Allegro, b. Andantino, c. Allegro. No. 3 in B flat minor, a. Allegro moderato, b. Andante, c. Allegretto.

68. Two Rondinos, 1912, UE. No. 1 in G sharp minor. No. 2 in C sharp minor.

74. Four lyric pieces, 1914, BH.
    1. Eclogue. 2. Soft West Wind. 3. At the Dance. 4. In the Old Home.

75. Five Pieces, 1914, H.
    1. When the Mountain-ash is in Flower. 2. The Lonely Fir. 3. The Aspen. 4. The Birch. 5. The Fir.

76. Thirteen Pieces, 1914 (?), H.
    1. Esquisse. 2. Étude. 3. Carillon. 4. Humoresque. 5. Consolation. 6. Romanzetta. 7. Affettuoso. 8. Pièce enfantine. 9. Arabesque. 10. Elegiaco. 11. Linnea. 12. Capricietto. 13. Harlequinade.

85. Five Pieces, 1916, H.
    1. Bellis. 2. Oeillet. 3. Iris. 4. Aquileja. 5. Campanula.

94. Six Pieces, 1919, W.
    1. Dance. 2. Novelette. 3. Sonnet. 4. Berger et Bergerette. 5. Mélodie. 6. Gavotte.

97. Six Bagatelles, 1920, BH.
    1. Humoresque I. 2. Song. 3. Little Waltz. 4. Humorous March. 5. Impromptu. 6. Humoresque II.

99. Eight Pieces, 1922, F.
    1. Pièce humoristique. 2. Esquisse. 3. Souvenir. 4. Impromptu. 5. Couplet. 6. Animoso. 7. Moment de Valse. 8. Petite Marche.

101. Five Pieces, 1923, H.
    1. Romance. 2. Chant de soir. 3. Scène lyrique. 4. Humoresque. 5. Scène romantiique.

103. Five Pieces, 1924, H.
    1. The Village Church. 2. The Fiddler. 3. The Oarsman. 4. The Storm. 5. In Mournful Mood.

114. *Esquisses*, Five Sketches, 1929, MS.
    1. Landscape. 2. Winter Scene. 3. Forest Lake. 4. Song in the Forest. 5. Spring Vision.

    Allegretto, 1889, MS.
    Andantino, 1888, MS.
    Au crépuscule, 1887, MS.
    Florestan, suite with descriptive text by the composer, 1889, MS.
    1. Moderato. 2. Molto moderato. 3. Andante. 4. Tempo primo.
    Kavaljeren (The Cavalier), 1900.
    Mandolinato, 1917, H.
    Morceau romantique sur un motif de M. Jacob de Julin, 1925, D.
    Scherzo, 1888 (?), MS.
    Spagnuolo, 1913.
    Till trånaden (To longing), 1913.

Choral Works and Cantatas

Opus
7. *Kullervo*, symphonic poem for soprano, baritone, male chorus and orchestra, 1892, MS.
    1. Introduction. 2. The Youth of Kullervo. 3. Kullervo and His Sister. 4. Kullervo Leaves for the War. 5. Kullervo's Death.
    2222/4331/11/0/str.
14. *Rakastava* (The lover), for male chorus *a cappella* with text from Book I of the *Kanteletar*, 1893, YL.
    1. *Missä armahani?* (Where is my beloved?). 2. *Armahan kulku* (My beloved's path). 3. *Hyvää iltaa, lintuseni* (Good evening, my little bird). For male chorus and string orchestra, 1894, MS. For mixed chorus *a cappella*, 1898, SÄV.
18. Nine Part-songs, for male chorus *a cappella*.
    1. *Isänmaalle* (To the fatherland) (Cajander), 1900, KO. Also known as *Yks' voima* (One power). 2. *Veljeni vierailla mailla* (My brothers abroad) (Aho), 1904, LM. 3. *Saarella palaa* (Fire on the island) (*Kanteletar*), 1895, BH. 4. *Min rastas raataa* (Busy as a thrush) (*Kanteletar*), 1898, SÄV. 5. *Metsämiehen laulu* (The woodman's song) (Kivi), 1898, BH. 6. *Sydämeni laulu* (The song of my heart) (Kivi), 1898, BH. 7. *Sortunut ääni* (The broken voice) (*Kanteletar*), 1898, BH. 8. *Terve kuu* (Hail, moon!) (*Kalevala*), 1901, BH. 9. *Venematka* (The boat journey) (*Kalevala*), 1893, BH. 1, 3, 4, 6, 7 and 9 also for mixed chorus *a cappella*.
19. *Impromptu*, for women's chorus and orchestra (Rydberg), 1902, rev. 1910, BH. Also known as *Lifslust* and *Gossar och flickor*.
    2222/4000/11/1/str.

21. *Natus in curas*, for male chorus *a capella* (Gustafsson), 1896, BH.
23. Cantata for the University Ceremonies of 1897, for soloists, mixed chorus and orchestra (Koskimies), 1897, MS. 1. *Me nuoriso Suomen* (We, the youth of Finland). 2. *Tuuli tuudittele* (The wind rocks). 3. *Oi toivo, toivo, sä lietomieli* (Oh Hope, Hope, you dreamer). 4. *Montapa elon merellä* (Many on the sea of life). 5. *Sammuva sainio maan* (The fading thoughts of the earth). 6a. *Soi kiitokseksi Luojan* (Let thanks ring unto the Lord). 6b. *Tuule, tuule leppeämmin* (Blow, blow gentler). 7. *Lempi, sun valtas ääretön on* (Love, your realm is limitless). 8. *Kuin virta vuolas* (As the swift current). 9. *Oi kallis Suomi, äiti verraton* (Oh, precious Finland, incomparable mother).
28. *Sandels*, improvisation for male chorus and orchestra (Runeberg), 1898, rev. 1915, MS. 2222/4230/11/0/str.
29. *Snöfrid*, improvisation for mixed chorus, recitation and orchestra (Rydberg), 1900 (?), MS. 2121/2310/11/0/str.
30. *Islossningen i Uleå alv* (The breaking of the ice on the Ulea River) (Topelius), improvisations for male chorus, recitation and orchestra, 1898, MS. 2222/4331/11/0/str.
31. 1. *Laulu Lemminkäiselle* (A song for Lemminkäinen) (Veijola), for male chorus and orchestra, 1894 (?), MS. 2222/4231/10/0/str.
    2. *Har du mod?* (Have you courage?) (Wecksell), for male chorus and orchestra, 1904, MS. 2222/4231/12/0/str.
    3. *Atenarnes sång* (song of the Athenians) (Rydberg), for boys' and men's voices with saxhorn septet and percussion, 1899, MS.
32. *Tulen synty* (The origin of fire) (Kalevala), for male chorus and orchestra, 1902, rev. 1910, MS. 2222/4231/13/0/str.
48. *Vapautettu kuningatar* (The liberated queen) (Cajander), cantata for mixed chorus and orchestra, 1906, L. 2222/4230/13/0/str.
65. Two Part-songs for mixed chorus *a cappella*; BH. 1. *Män från slätten och havet* (People from land and sea) (Knape), 1911. 2. *Bell Melody of Kallio Church* (Engström), 1912.
84. Five Part-songs for male chorus *a cappella*: 1. *Herr Lager* (Fröding), 1914, MM. 2. *På berget* (On the mountain) (Gripenberg), 1915, MM. 3. *Ett drömackord* (A dream chord) (Fröding), 1915, MM. 4. *Evige Eros* (Eternal Eros) (Gripenberg), 1915, MM. 5. *Till havs* (At sea) (Reuter), 1915, W.
91. 1. *March of the Finnish Jaeger Battalion* (Nurmio), 1917, BH. For male chorus *a cappella* and for male chorus with orchestra. 2232/4330/12/0/str.
    2. *Scout March* (Finne-Procopé), for mixed chorus *a cappella*. Also with orchestra, 1917, H. 2222/4331/10/0/str. Also known as *Det danske Spejderes March* (The Danish scout march) and The World Song of the World Association of Girl Guides and Girl Scouts.

92. *Oma maa* (Our native land) (Kallio), cantata for mixed chorus and orchestra, 1918, W. 2222/4230/11/0/str.
93. *Jordens sång* (Song of the earth) (Hemmer), cantata for mixed chorus and orchestra, 1919, MS. 2222/3220/10/0/str.
95. *Maan virsi* (Hymn of the earth) (Eino Leino), cantata for mixed chorus and orchestra, 1920, W. 2222/4230/10/0/str.
107. Hymn, for chorus with organ, 1925, MS (?).
108. Two Part-songs, for male chorus *a cappella* (Larin-Kyösti), 1925, LM.
    1. Humoreski. 2. *Ne pitkän matkan kulkijat* (Wanderers on the long way).
110. *Väinön virsi* (Väinö's song) (Kalevala), for mixed chorus and orchestra, 1926, W. 2222/4330/11/0/str.

Aamusumussa (Morning mist) (Erkko), for three children's voices *a cappella*. Also for male and mixed chorus, 1896, KO. Also known as *Päiv' ei pääse*. *Brusande rusar en våg* (The roaring of a wave) (Schybergson), for male chorus *a cappella*, 1918, W.

Cantata for the coronation of Nicolas II (Cajander), for soloists, mixed chorus and orchestra, 1896, MS (?).

Cantata to words by Walter von Konow, for women's chorus *a cappella*, 1911, A.

Cantata for the University Ceremonies of 1894 (Kasimir Leino), for mixed chorus and orchestra, 1894, MS. 2222/2221/12/0/str.

Drömmarna (Dreams) (Reuter), for mixed chorus *a cappella*, 1912, SFV. Ej med klagan (Not with lamentations) (Runeberg), for mixed chorus *a cappella*, 1905, SAV. Also known as *Till minnet av Albert Edelfelt* (To the memory of Albert Edelfelt).

Fridolins dårskap (Fridolin's Folly) (Karlfeldt), for male chorus *a cappella*, 1917, AH.

Johdantovuorolauluja, Introductory Antiphons for mixed chorus, 1925, WS. 1. Palmusunnuntaina (Palm Sunday). 2. Pyhäinpäivänä (All Saints' Day). 3. Rukouspäivänä (General prayers).

Jone Havsfärd (Jonah's Voyage) (Karlfeldt), for male chorus *a cappella*, 1918, WS. Published as *Joonaan Meriretki* (Nortamo).

Kansakoululaisten marssi (School children's march) (Onnen Pekka), for children's voices *a cappella*, 1910. Also known as *Uno Cygnæuksen muistolle* (to the memory of Uno Cygnæus).

Karjalan Osa (Karelia's fate) (Nurminen), march for male chorus with piano, 1930, MK. Also known as *Isänmaallinen marssi* (Patriotic march).

Kotikaipaus (Nostalgia) (von Konow), for three women's voices *a cappella*, 1902, SM.

Koulutie (the way to school) (Koskenniemi), for children's voices *a cappella*, 1925, WS.

Kuutamolla (In the moonlight) (Suonio), for male chorus *a cappella*, 1916, YL.

Likhet (Resemblance) (Runeberg), for male chorus *a cappella*, 1922, MA.

Siltavahti (The guard of the bridge) (Sola), for male chorus *a cappella*, 1929, JW.

Suur' olet, Herra (You are mighty, oh Lord) (Korpela), hymn for mixed chorus *a cappella*, 1927, SL. For male chorus LM.

Till Thérèse Hahl (To Thérèse Hahl) (Tavaststjerna), for mixed chorus *a cappella*, 1902, SÄV.

Työkansan marssi (Workers' march) (Erkko), for mixed chorus *a cappella*, 1893–6.

Ute hörs stormen (One hears the storm outside) (Schybergson), for male chorus *a cappella*, 1918, W.

Uusmaalaisten laulu (Song for the people of Uusimaa) (Terhi), for mixed chorus *a cappella*, 1912, KO. Also for male chorus.

Viipurin Laulu-Veikkojen kunniamarssi (Honour march of the singing brothers of Viipuri) (Eerola), for male chorus *a cappella*, 1920, JW.

For Solo Voice with Orchestra

Opus

3. *Arioso* (Runeberg), song with string orchestra, 1893, rev. 1913, W.
13. Seven Songs of Runeberg, with piano, BH.
    4. *Våren flyktar hastigt* (Spring is flying), 1891, 1914, MS. 2000/4000/01/0/str.
17. Seven Songs, with piano, BH.
    1. *Se'n har jag ej frågat mera* (And I questioned then no further) (Runeberg), 1894, 1903, MS. 2222/4000/11/0/str. 2. *Sov in!* (Slumber) (Tavaststjerna), 1894, MS. 2022/1000/10/0/str. 3. Fågellek (Enticement) (Tavaststjerna), 1891, MS. 1100/1000/01/1/str. 5. *En slända* (The dragonfly) (Levertin), 1894 (?), MS. 2122/3000/01/1/str.
33. *Koskenlaskijan morsiamet* (The Rapids-shooter's brides) (Oksanen), for baritone or mezzo-soprano and orchestra, 1897, BH. 2222/4230/13/0/str.
35. Two Songs, with piano, 1907–8, BH.
    1. *Jubal* (Josephson), MS. 2122/2000/01/1/str.
36. Six Songs, with piano, 1899, BH.
    3. *Bollspelet vid Trianon* (Tennis at Trianon) (Fröding), MS. 2011/0000/01/1/str.

6. *Demanten på marssnön* (The diamond on the March snow) (Weck-sell), MS. 2020/0000/00/1/str.

37. Five Songs, with piano, BH.
    3. Soluppgång (Sunrise) (Hedberg), 1898, MS. 2022/4000/10/0/str.
    5. *Flickan kom ifrån sin älsklings möte* (The maiden came from her lover's tryst) (Runeberg), 1901, MS. 1122/2030/11/1/ str.

38. Five Songs, with piano, BH.
    1. *Höstkväll* (Autumn evening) (Rydberg), 1903. 0233/4030/10/1/ str. 2. *På verandan vid havet* (On a balcony by the sea) (Rydberg), 1902, MS. 0222/4000/01/1/str. 3. *I natten* (In the night) (Rydberg), 1903, MS. 0012/4000/11/0/str.

50. Six Songs, with piano, 1906, L.
    4. *Aus banger Brust* (Oh, wert thou here) (Dehmel), MS. 1012/ 2000/00/1/str.

70. *Luonnotar* (Spirit of nature) (*Kalevala*), tone-poem for soprano and orchestra, 1913, MS. 2232/4230/20/2/str.
    Serenade (Stagnelius), for baritone with orchestra, 1895, MS. 0222/4000/00/0/str.

Songs with Piano Accompaniment

Opus

1. Five Christmas Songs, 1895–1913, W.
   1. *Nu står jul vid snöig port* (Now Christmas stands at the snowy gate) (Topelius). 2. *Nu så kommer julen* (Now Christmas comes) (Topelius). 3. *Det mörknar ute* (Outside it grows dark) (Topelius). 4. *Giv mig ej glans* (Give me no splendour) (Topelius). 5. *On hanget korkeat* (High are the snowdrifts) (Joukahainen).

3. *Arioso* (Runeberg), 1893, rev. 1913, W.

13. Seven Songs (Runeberg), BH.
    1. *Under strandens granar* (Neath the fir trees), 1892. 2. *Kyssens hopp* (The kiss's hope), 1892. 3. *Hjärtats morgon* (The heart's morning), 1891. 4. *Våren flyktar hastigt* (Spring is flying), 1891. 5. *Drömmen* (The dream), 1891. 6. *Till Frigga* (To Frigga), 1892. 7. *Jägargossen* (The young hunter), 1891.

17. Seven Songs, BH.
    1. *Se'n har jag ej frågat mera* (And I questioned no further), (Runeberg), 1894. 2. *Sov in!* (Slumber) (Tavaststjerna), 1894. 3. *Fågellek* (Enticement) (Tavaststjerna), 1891. 4. *Vilse* (Astray) (Tavaststjerna), 1894. 5. *En slända* (The dragonfly) (Levertin), 1894 (?). 6. *Illalle* (To Ilta) (Forsman-Koskimies), 1898. 7. *Lastu lainehilla* (Driftwood) (Calamnius), 1898.

35. Two Songs, 1907–8, BH.
    1. *Jubal* (Josephson). 2. *Teodora* (Gripenberg).

36. Six Songs, 1899, BH.
   1. *Svarta rosor* (Black roses) (Josephson). 2. *Men min fågel märks dock icke* (But my bird is long in homing) (Runeberg). 3. *Bollspelet vid Trianon* (Tennis at Trianon) (Fröding). 4. *Säv, säv, susa* (Sigh, sedges, sigh) (Fröding). 5. *Marssnön* (March snow) (Wecksell). 6. *Demanten på marssönn* (Wecksell).

37. Five Songs, BH.
   1. *Den första kyssen* (The first kiss) (Runeberg), 1898. 2. *Lasse liten* (Little Lasse) (Topelius), 1898. 3. *Soluppgång* (Sunrise) (Hedberg), 1898. 4. *Var det en dröm?* (Was it a dream?) (Wecksell), 1902. 5. *Flickan kom ifrån sin älsklings möte* (The maiden came from her lover's tryst) (Runeberg), 1901.

38. Five Songs, BH.
   1. *Höstkväll* (Autumn evening) (Rydberg), 1903. 2. *På verandan vid havet* (On a balcony by the sea) (Rydberg), 1902. 3. *I natten* (In the night) (Rydberg), 1903. 4. *Harpolekaren och hans son* (The harper and his son) (Rydberg), 1904. 5. *Jag ville jag vore i Indialand* (I wish I dwelt in India) (Fröding), 1904.

50. Six Songs, 1906, L.
   1. *Lenzgesang* (Spring song) (Fitger). 2. *Sehnsucht* (Longing) (Weiss). 3. *Im Feld ein Mädchen singt* (In the field a maiden sings) (Susman). 4. *Aus banger Brust* (Oh, wert thou here) (Dehmel). 5. *Die stille Stadt* (The silent city) (Dehmel). 6. *Rosenlied* (Song of the roses) (Ritter).

57. Eight Songs (Josephson), 1909, L.
   1. *Älvan och snigeln* (The fairy and the snail). 2. *En blomma stod vid vägen* (A flower stood by the path). 3. *Kvarnhjulet* (The millwheel). 4. *Maj* (May). 5. *Jag är ett träd* (I am a tree). 6. *Hertig Magnus* (Duke Magnus). 7. *Vänskapens blomma* (The flower of friendship). 8. *Näcken* (The watersprite).

61. Eight Songs, 1910, BH.
   1. *Långsamt som kvällskyn* (Slowly as the evening sun) (Tavaststjerna). 2. *Vattenplask* (Lapping waters) (Rydberg). 2. *När jag drommer* (When I dream) (Tavaststjerna). 4. *Romeo* (Tavaststjerna). 5. *Romance* (Tavaststjerna). 6. *Dolce far niente* (Tavaststjerna). 7. *Fåfäng onskan* (Idle wish) (Runeberg). 8. *Vårtagen* (Spell of springtime) (Gripenberg).

72. Six Songs.
   1. *Vi ses igen* (Farewell) (Rydberg), 1914, MS lost. 2. *Orions bälte* (Orion's girdle) (Topelius), 1914, MS lost. 3. *Kyssen* (The kiss) (Rydberg), 1915, BH. 4. *Kaiutar* (The echo nymph) (Larin Kyösti), 1915, BH. 5. *Der Wanderer und der Bach* (The wanderer and the brook) (Greif), 1915, BH. 6. *Hundra vägar* (A hundred ways) (Runeberg), 1907, BH.

86. Six Songs, 1916, H.
  1. *Vårförnimmelser* (The coming of spring) (Tavaststjerna).
  2. *Längtan heter min arvedel* (Longing is my heritage) (Karlfeldt).
  3. *Dold förening* (Hidden union) (Snoilsky). 4. *Och finns det en
  tanke* (And is there a thought?) (Tavaststjerna). 5. *Sångarlön*
  The singer's reward (Snoilsky). 6. *I systrar, I bröder* (Ye sisters,
  ye brothers) (Lybeck).
88. Six Songs (1–3 Franzén, 4–6 Runeberg), 1917, H.
  1. *Blåsippan* (The blue anemone). 2. *De bägge rosorna* (The two
  roses). 3. *Vitsippan* (The star-flower). 4. *Sippan* (The anemone).
  5. *Törnet* (The thorn). 6. *Blommans öde* (The flower's destiny).
90. Six Songs (Runeberg), 1917, BH.
  1. *Norden* (The north). 2. *Hennes budskap* (Her message). 3. *Mor-
  gonen* (The morning). 4. *Fågelfängaren* (The bird-catcher).
  5. *Sommarnatten* (Summer night). 6. *Vem styrde hit din väg?*
  (Who has brought you here?).
  Erloschen (Lost) (Busse-Palmo), 1906, SM.
  Hymn to Thaïs (Borgström), 1900, MS.
  Narciss (Gripenberg), 1918 (?), W.
  Segelfahrt/Sailing (Öhquist), 1899.
  Serenade (Runeberg), 1888.
  Små flickorna (Small girls) (Procopé), 1920.
  Souda, souda, sinisorsa (Swim, swim, duck) (Koskimies), 1899, F.

Miscellaneous Works

Opus
15. *Skogsrået* (The wood-nymph), melodrama for piano, two horns and
  strings to accompany the recitation of verses by Rydberg, 1894,
  MS.
111. Two Pieces for Organ, W.
  1. *Intrada*, 1925. 2. *Surusoitto* (Funeral music), 1931.
113. Masonic Ritual Music, for male voices, piano and organ, 1927,
  1938 and 1946, M.
  1. Introduction. 2. Thoughts be our Comfort (Schiller). 3. Introduction and Hymn (Confucius). 4. Marcia (Goethe). 5. Light
  (Simelius), 6. Salem, also: Onward ye Peoples (Rydberg),
  7. Whosoever Hath a Love (Rydberg). 8. Ode to Fraternity
  (Sario). 9. Hymn (Sario). 10. Marche Funèbre. 11. Ode (Korpela). 12. Finlandia Hymn (Sola).

  Carminalia, Latin songs for students arranged for soprano, alto and
  bass *a cappella* or soprano and alto with piano and harmonium,
  from melodies and texts collected by Elise Stenback, 1899, KW.
  1. *Ecce novum gaudium.* 2. *Angelus emittitur.* 3. *In stadio laboris.*

Ett ensamt skidspår (The lonely ski trail), for piano to accompany the recitation of verses by Bertel Gripenberg, 1925, NMF. Same for harp and string orchestra, 1948, MS.

Finnish Folk Songs, arranged for piano, 1903, BH.
1. *Minun kultani* (My beloved). 2. *Sydämestäni rakastan* (I love you with all my heart). 3. *Ilta tulee* (Evening comes). 4. *Tuopa tyttö, kaunis tyttö* (That beautiful girl). 5. *Velisurmaaja* (The brother's murderer). 6. *Häämuistelma* (Wedding memory).

Finnish Runos (Kalevala), seventeen fragments, 1895.

Grefvinnans konterfej (The countess's portrait), for string orchestra to accompany the recitation of verses by Z. Topelius, 1906, MS. Also:
Porträtterna (The portraits).

Herran siunaus (God's blessing), hymn with organ, 1925, WS.

Jungfrun i tornet (The maid in the tower), opera in one act (Herzberg), 1896, MS. 1121/2110/01/0/str.

Kehtolaulu (Lullaby), for violin and kantele, 1899.

Näcken (The watersprite), two songs for the fairy-tale play by G. Wennerberg, 1888, MS.

Svartsjukans nätter (Nights of jealousy), for violin, cello and piano to accompany the recitation of verses by Runeberg, 1888, MS.

Tanken (The thought) (Runeberg), duet for two sopranos with piano, 1915, MS.

Three Songs for American schools, 1913, SB.
1. Autumn Song (Dixon). 2. The Sun upon the Lake is Low (Scott). 3. A Cavalry Catch (Macleod).

Tiera, tone-poem for brass ensemble and percussion, 1898, KO.

Trånaden (Longing), for piano to accompany the recitation of verses by Stagnelius, 1887, MS.

Translations of titles of works are subject to some variation according to context. In the Discography titles have been given as they appear in the standard British catalogues. It will be found that the Schwann Catalogue (U.S.A.) shows still other forms. In no case, however, does difficulty arise over identification.

SIBELIUS AND THE GRAMOPHONE

ᗒᗒ

Introduction

Sibelius has been well served by the record industry since the early 1930s when electrical recording really got into its stride. Robert Kajanus, the first great Sibelius interpreter, came to London in 1930 to record the First and Second Symphonies for the then Columbia Gramophone Company, later part of EMI. By 1932 The Gramophone Company Ltd, on its HMV label, had launched the Sibelius Society which offered records covering a large section from Sibelius's output on a subscription basis. Kajanus subsequently made records for the Society of the Third Symphony, *Tapiola* and *Pohjola's Daughter*. These records remained a touchstone of Sibelius interpretation for many years. Among other conductors involved were Sir Thomas Beecham, Sir Adrian Boult, Serge Koussevitzky and Georg Schnéevoigt, the last named a Finn regarded by some as superior to Kajanus. The most significant contribution was perhaps Beecham's, whose records included not only the Violin Concerto with Heifetz as soloist but also the Fourth Symphony, *En Saga*, some of *The Tempest* music and rarities like *The Bard*. Koussevitzky was represented by the Seventh Symphony, recorded in public by the B.B.C. Symphony Orchestra in the Queen's Hall. For RCA Victor in the U.S.A., this outstanding Sibelius conductor made, with the Boston Symphony Orchestra, the Second and Fifth Symphonies in addition to *Pohjola's Daughter* and *Tapiola*. These were without doubt some of the most exciting Sibelius performances of all time. With the Philadelphia Orchestra, Leopold Stokowski and later Eugene Ormandy also made significant additions to the catalogue of Sibelius records during the 78-r.p.m. era.

With the advent of long-playing records, the first complete cycle of the symphonies, performed by the London Symphony Orchestra under Anthony Collins, came from Decca. There was also a set by Sixten Ehrling and the Stockholm Philharmonic Orchestra, published on the American Mercury label. Individual records of various symphonies came from Beecham, Herbert von Karajan, Paul Kletzki and Ormandy. The stereophonic age has brought complete versions of the symphonies from several sources, notably Sir John Barbirolli and the Hallé Orchestra (HMV), Leonard Bernstein and the New York Philharmonic (CBS—USA), Lorin Maazel and the Vienna Philharmonic Orchestra (Decca) and even from Japan, with the Japan Philharmonic Orchestra conducted by Akeo Watanabe. Karajan, with the Berlin Philharmonic (DGG), has recorded Nos. 4, 5, 6 and 7 and there have been important records from artists like Ernest Anseimet, Tauno Hannikainen, Sir Malcolm Sargent and George Szell.

Although performances of Sibelius's music are comparatively infrequent, all available evidence points to his continued popularity as far as record collectors are concerned. There are currently at least four thoroughly recommendable versions of the forbidding A minor Symphony; Sibelius in his most serious mood may not be to everybody's taste but according to the B.B.C.'s 'Hundred Best Tunes', the No. 1 spot is occupied by *Finlandia*! Even *Luonnotar*, long thought to be an unbridgeable gap, has been recorded and as these notes are written, the world première recording of *Kullervo* has recently been published. The major omission remains the complete incidental music for *The Tempest*, but as record companies now have a commendable habit of making 'complete versions' it can only be a matter of time before this gap is filled.

DOUGLAS PUDNEY
London, October 1971

Notes on discography
The discography listed below does not set out to be a complete one but is selective. At the time it was compiled the majority of the records were readily available in the United Kingdom. As record companies' catalogues are subject to change through addition and deletion, and these days through reissues at various price levels, the picture could well be very different within a short time.

A SELECT DISCOGRAPHY

Symphonies

Kullervo Symphony Op. 7—(with 'Swan- HMV SLS 807   1970
white' excerpts from incidental music; (2 records)
'Scene with Cranes' from 'Kuolema')
Paavo Berglund/Bournemouth Symphony
Orchestra; soloists and Helsinki Male
Voice Choir

Symphony No. 1 in E minor, Op. 39
Sir John Barbirolli/The Hallé Orchestra HMV ASD 2366   1967
(*with* 'Pelléas and Mélisande' excerpts)
Carl   Garaguly/Dresden   Philharmonic Philips SFM 23000 1965
Orchestra (*with* Symphony No. 7)
Lorin Maazel/Vienna Philharmonic Orches- Decca SXL 6084   1963
tra (*with* 'Karelia Suite')

Symphony No. 2 in D major, Op. 43
Sir John Barbirolli/The Hallé Orchestra HMV ASD 2308   1963
(*with* 'The Swan of Tuonela')
Sir Thomas Beecham/B.B.C. Symphony World Record Club
Orchestra. (B.B.C. recording of public ST 1085 (Electronic
performance, Royal Festival Hall 1954) stereo)
Tauno Hannikainen/Sinfonia of London World Record Club
ST 33   1957

Serge Koussevitzky/Boston Symphony Or- RCA VIC 1186
chestra (LP transfer of 78 rpm
recording originally made
in 1950)

George Szell/Amsterdam Concertgebow Or- Philips SAL 3515 1964
chestra

Symphony No. 3 in C major, Op. 52
Sir John Barbirolli/The Hallé Orchestra   HMV ASD 2648   1970
(*with* Symphony No. 6)
Lorin Maazel/Vienna Philharmonic Orches-   Decca SXL 6364   1968
tra (*with* Symphony No. 6)

Symphony No. 4 in A minor, Op. 63
Sir John Barbirolli/The Hallé Orchestra   HMV ASD 2494   1969
(*with* Rakastava; Romance in C)
Sir Thomas Beecham/London Philharmonic   World Record Club
(*with* The Bard; In Memoriam and Lem-   SH 133
minkainen's Homeward Journey)   (LP transfer of 78 rpm
recording originally made
in 1937)

Paavo Berglund/Helsinki Radio Symphony   Decca International
Orchestra (*with* Mauermusik by Sallinen)   SXL 6431   1968
Tauno Hannikainen/USSR State Symphony   Mezhdunarodnaya Kniga
Orchestra   —USSR 04794–5
(mono only)   *c.* 1950
Herbert von Karajan/Berlin Philharmonic   Deutsche Grammophon
Orchestra (*with* The Swan of Tuonela)   138974   1965
Lorin Maazel/Vienna Philharmonic Orches-   Decca SXL 6365   1968
tra (*with* Tapiola)

Symphony No. 5 in E flat major, Op. 82
Sir John Barbirolli/The Hallé Orchestra   HMV ASD 2326   1967
(*with* Symphony No. 7)
Tauno Hannikainen/Sinfonia of London   World Record Club
(*with* Karelia Suite)   ST 42   1958
Herbert von Karajan/Berlin Philharmonic   Deutsche Grammophon
Orchestra (*with* Tapiola)   SLPH 138973   1965
Lorin Maazel/Vienna Philharmonic Orches-   Decca SXL 6236   1965
tra (*with* Symphony No. 7)

Symphony No. 6 in D minor, Op. 104
Sir John Barbirolli/The Hallé Orchestra   HMV ASD 2648   1970
(*with* Symphony No. 3)
Herbert von Karajan/Berlin Philharmonic   DGG 139032   1968
Orchestra (*with* Symphony No. 7)
Lorin Maazel/Vienna Philharmonic Orches-   Decca SXL 6364   1968
tra (*with* Symphony No. 3)

Symphony No. 7 in C major, Op. 105
Sir John Barbirolli/The Hallé Orchestra   HMV ASD 2326   1967
(*with* Symphony No. 5)

N.B.: The Barbirolli-Hallé performances of the seven symphonies are
also available as a box set of five records, with a booklet containing notes
and analyses by Robert Layton—HMV SLS 799.

Sir Thomas Beecham/Royal Philharmonic Orchestra (*with* Pelléas and Mélisande excerpts; The Oceanides)	HMV ASD 468	1957
Herbert von Karajan/Berlin Philharmonic Orchestra (*with* Symphony No. 6)	DGG 139032	1968
Lorin Maazel/Vienna Philharmonic Orchestra (*with* Symphony No. 5)	Decca SXL 6236	1965

Violin Concerto in D minor, Op. 47

David Oistrakh/Moscow Radio Symphony Orchestra/Gennady Rozhdestvensky (*with* Two Humoresques, Belshazzar's Feast, Romance in C)	HMV ASD 2407	1965
Kyung Wha Chung/London Symphony Orchestra/Andre Previn (*with* Tchaikovsky Violin Concerto)	Decca SXL 6493	1970
Jascha Heifetz/Chicago Symphony Orchestra/Walter Hendl	RCA SB 2101	1960
Tossy Spivakovsky/London Symphony Orchestra/Tauno Hannikainnen (*with* Tapiola)	Everest SDBR 3045	1960

Collections of Orchestral Music

Finlandia, Op. 26 Lemminkäinen's Homeward Journey, Op. 22 Karelia Suite, Op. 11 Valse Triste from 'Kuolema', Op. 44 Pohjola's Daughter, Op. 49 Sir John Barbirolli/The Hallé Orchestra	HMV ASD 2272	1966
Luonnotar Op. 70 En Saga, Op. 9 Nightride and Sunrise, Op. 55 The Oceanides, Op. 73 Antal Dorati/London Symphony Orchestra/ Gwyneth Jones	HMV ASD 2486	1969
Karelia Overture, Op. 10 King Christian II—Incidental Music Op. 27 Festivo Op. 25—No. 3 of Scènes Historiques The Bard, Op. 64 Alexander Gibson/Scottish National Orchestra	HMV HQS 1070	1966

Four Legends from the Kalevala. Op. 22
1. Lemminkäinen and the Maidens of Saari

2. The Swan of Tuonela
3. Lemminkäinen in Tuonela
4. Lemminkäinen's Homeward Journey

Lukas Foss/ Buffalo Philharmonic Orchestra	Nonesuch H 71203	1968
Thomas Jensen/Danish State Radio Symphony Orchestra	Decca ACL 138	1952
Tauno Hannikainen/USSR Radio Symphony Orchestra	Mezhdunarodnaya Kniga —USSR 04726-7 c 1950	

The Swan of Tuonela, Op. 22
Finlandia, Op. 26
Tapiola, Op. 112
Valse Triste, Op. 44

Herbert von Karajan/Berlin Philharmonic Orchestra	Deutsche Grammophon 139016	1967

Songs

Orchestrated by Sibelius
Arioso, Op. 3; Våren flyktar hastigt, Op. 13
No. 4; S'en har jag ej frågat mera, Op. 17
No. 1; Demanten på marssnön, Op. 36
No. 6; Höstkväll, Op. 38 No. 1; På
verandan vid havet, Op. 38 No. 2; Kom nu
hit, död!, Op. 60 No. 1

Orchestrated by other hands
Illalle, Op. 17 No. 6; Svarta rosor, Op.
36 No. 1; Men min fågel märks dock
icke, Op. 36 No. 2; Säv, säv, susa, Op. 36
No. 4; Den första kyssen, Op. 37 No. 1;
Var det en dröm?, Op. 37 No. 4; Flickan
kom ifrån sin älsklings möte, Op. 37 No. 5

Kirsten Flagstad/London Symphony Orchestra/Øivin Fjeldstad	Decca SDD 248	1958

N.B. Most of the hundred or so solo songs by Sibelius are settings of
Swedish lyrics. Swedish was long the second language of the
Finnish intelligentsia. On the other hand, Sibelius chose the
Finnish of the epic poetry for choral works and as an inspiration for
his orchestral tone-poems.

Index